FAITHFUL
ENDURANCE

CHRIST-CENTERED ENCOURAGEMENT
TO HELP YOU FIGHT
THE GOOD FIGHT OF FAITH

BILLY LONG

HIGH BRIDGE
BOOKS & MEDIA

Faithful Endurance
by Billy Long

Copyright © 2024 Billy Long

Printed in the United States of America
ISBN: 978-1-962802-05-5

All Scripture is taken from the New King James Version®. Copyright © 1982 by Thomas Nelson. Used by permission. All rights reserved.

High Bridge Books titles may be purchased in bulk for educational, business, fundraising, or sales promotional use. For information, please contact High Bridge Books via www.HighBridgeBooks.com/contact.

Published in Houston, Texas, by High Bridge Books.

Contents

Part One: Words of Encouragement _____ 1

1. God Controls the "All" and the "Each" _____ 3

2. A Special Treat _____ 7

3. An Encouraging Word _____ 9

4. Mistakes Are Part of Growth _____ 11

5. Dealing with Stumbles and Failures _____ 15

6. Dealing with Regrets _____ 19

7. Did I "Miss It"? _____ 21

8. He Would Have Passed Them By? _____ 25

9. The Struggle to Find Comfort _____ 29

10. Facing Eternity _____ 33

11. In Whose Hands? _____ 39

12. Misinterpreting God's Special Attention _____ 43

13. He Will Not Say, "Hey, You." _____ 47

14. Holy, but Not Silent _____ 51

15. "Behold, You Are There." _____ 55

Part Two: The Spiritual Battle _____ 57

16. Courage to Face the Battle _____ 59

17. "If There's Snakes in There, There's Fish in There." _____ 63

18. Standing Together in the Battle _____ 67

19. The Ugly Bug on the Wall _____ 71

20. It's Not Safe to Quit _____ 75

21. Suffering … or Inconvenience? _____77

22. The Enraged World _____81

23. Exorcism in the New Testament Church _____87

24. Qualities of the Effective Intercessor _____93

25. Some Keys to Successful Spiritual Warfare _____97

26. Our Disposition During Persecution _____105

Part Three: Some Stories and Testimonies _____113

27. Healed of Obsessive-Compulsive Disorder _____115

28. God's Provision for an Unusual Trip _____121

29. Aunt Ider _____125

30. Mama _____129

31. The Good Old Days and Wonderful Tomorrow ___131

32. L.D. and the Religious Folk _____135

33. Fragrance_____139

34. My Visit to a Philosophy of Religion Class _____141

Part Four: Warnings _____145

35. Your Sins Will Find You Out_____147

36. Lessons from Jonah _____151

37. Lust and Temptation _____157

38. Lust and Lures _____161

39. Lust and Snares _____163

40. Disobey and Have a Party_____165

Part Five: Personal Integrity _____167

41. Disillusionment: Blinded by Your Limited "Now" Perspective __169

42. Advice to the Woman Looking for a Good Man ___173

43. The Fly in the Ointment _____177

44. Waiting for God to Judge _____ 181

45. The Hard Heart _____ 187

46. Icy Hot _____ 191

47. Practical Wisdom and Being Led by the Holy Spirit _____ 195

48. Forgiveness _____ 199

49. Being Genuine _____ 203

Part Six: Cultural Issues _____ 207

50. Abortion: Brutality, Loss of Natural Affection, and
    Child Sacrifice _____ 209

51. God and Creation _____ 219

52. Calling Evil Good and Good Evil _____ 225

53. Means of Deception _____ 229

54. Loyalty Issues _____ 235

55. Manipulation and Control _____ 239

56. Perspective on Grace, Works, Faith, Obedience,
    and Repentance _____ 245

57. Trusting God's Wisdom and Love _____ 251

Part One

Words of Encouragement

1

God Controls the "All" and the "Each"

F OR THOSE SPIRITUAL VETERANS WHO HAVE BEEN THROUGH TRI-
als, disillusionment, and disappointments, this chapter is written to encour-
age you to persevere and stand in faith, trusting God's ability to perform His
will in your life as you surrender to Him in faith and obedience.

Facing discouragement and seeing the failures of God's people, we are
often tempted to lose heart and faith. We have seen what we thought were
the wrong people succeeding and the wrong people failing. Like John the
Baptist, we have seen the glory and said, "Behold! The Lamb of God!" Then
we sat in our "prison cells" and said, "Are you the one or do we look for
another? Did I miss it?"

We stood on the mountain top and cried out, "This is it!" And we
crawled on the valley floor, crying, "Where did it go?" We said, "Lord, I'll
never leave You nor forsake You," and later denied Him before the rooster
crowed. We slept while others were in their Gethsemanes. We have had
friends walk into our Gethsemanes and betray us with a kiss. We have seen
churches fly and churches fall. We have been in the processes of God and
were not sure whether we were being pruned or stripped, whether we were
being purged and refined or burned and rejected. In our attempts at obedience, we have at times stepped out in faith, not sure whether we were stepping up or stepping off. We fell asleep in the boat during the storm and did
not know whether to stand up and say, "Peace! Be still!" or whether to ask
someone to throw us overboard to the whale.

During all of the situations above, it is easy to lose sight of the fact that
the eternal purpose of God was accomplished in Christ Jesus our Lord
(Eph. 3:11). Instead of being in the pits of unbelief because of our failures

or that of others, we should rejoice that Almighty God will complete the Church and bring forth His kingdom. Not one jot or tittle shall fail of what He has said regarding the Church and His kingdom plan. Jesus, while hanging on the cross, gored by the "bulls of Bashan," bitten by demonic dogs, and "pierced by the congregation of the wicked" (Ps. 22) which surrounded Him on Calvary, could still, in the face of this, know that all things were accomplished and that the Scripture concerning Himself had been fulfilled. He thus could say, "It is finished!" (John 19:25–30). How much more now from His place of glory and authority at the right hand of the Father, even in the face of a hostile world and a stubborn and stiff-necked Church, will He not again come to say in the proper time, "It is finished"?

The book of Ephesians speaks of God's purpose, God's people, God's grace, and God's power. These are high and lofty elements; they represent the wonderful work of God. The book also deals with the nitty-gritty areas of life such as unity, godly living, spiritual warfare, the family, relationships, etc. Sooner or later, God's purpose, power, and grace will prevail in the nitty-gritty, and God will reveal in His people just how much He really is able to do exceedingly, abundantly above all that we can ask or think (Eph. 3:20). He is able to subdue all things unto Himself (Phil. 3:21). He will complete His work.

We have faith for the past and for the future—but we think God has trouble handling the present. We believe God controls all things. He controls the whole—but we think He has difficulty with the parts and the particulars. We believe He sets the boundaries of nations—but we think He has no control over the unreasonable and trespassing neighbor who has moved the boundary lines of our front yard. We believe, according to the Scripture, that God will produce the glorious Church, that He will succeed with the whole—but we think He is failing with the parts, with the individuals, and that He controls the "whole" but not the "each." Obviously, we must realize that to determine the boundaries of nations, God must have power over the neighbor's small plot. To be God of history, He must also be God of the moment. To control past and future, He must control the present. He is God over all. He will complete His work and fulfill His counsel. Not one jot or tittle shall fail of all His good promises.

The Apostle Paul experienced every type of evil from the hands of men, including attempts to destroy his life. He experienced grief from the failures of churches under his ministry. He was forsaken and rejected. He even suffered at the hands of the demonic messenger of Satan sent to buffet him. Yet despite all this, he spoke eloquently and with great faith concerning God's plan for the Church. He trusted in God, in God's wisdom and power. Paul began the book of Ephesians with the phrase, "Paul ... an apostle by the will of God" (Eph. 1:1). Having experienced God's sovereign initiative and power and having seen how it completely transformed him into God's faithful and passionate servant, Paul basically proceeded to say, both explicitly and implicitly in the book of Ephesians, that the Church, the people of God, will also be transformed and made into the perfect man by the same will of God and by the same power of God.

God is building together a people into a habitation of God through the Spirit. That People is His heritage, His chosen possession, through which His great power and grace shall be demonstrated, through which the manifold wisdom of God shall be made manifest unto principalities and powers, and through which His life and image shall be reflected upon the Earth. His kingdom shall come. He shall bring down all principalities and powers until His enemies are made a footstool for His feet. His glory shall cover the earth as the waters cover the sea.

Therefore, we should not be moved away from the hope (the confident expectation) of the fulfillment of all that is promised and proclaimed in the gospel. The Sovereign God is administrating times and seasons, each to its fullness, until all things are fulfilled in Christ. God's sovereignty, His power, His grace, and His wisdom are the backdrop and foundation for our faith and confidence. There is no place to sit down disillusioned with God, His purpose, His plan, or His Church. God is able and will do exceedingly, abundantly above all we can ask or think. No matter how discouraging our own experiences have been, God will succeed. The eternal purpose of God the Father was accomplished in Christ Jesus our Lord (Eph. 3:11).

Why are you cast down, O my soul? Hope in God. (Ps. 42:11)

2

A Special Treat

I HAVE SPOKEN TWICE AT THE RECOVERY CHURCH IN CHARLOTTE, North Carolina, where Jim Shock is the pastor. An amazing thing happened both times I was there.

During my first visit, before I began my message, one of their members named David went to the podium and read a Scripture and said a few words before taking up the offering. The amazing thing is that the very verse he read was my text for the morning message, and my Bible was open to that very verse. Without realizing it, he had chosen a Bible verse that just happened to be the topic of my message. When I stood up to speak, I told him and the congregation how he had been led by the Spirit to select the very verse that I was about to speak on and that his word had confirmed the message I was about to bring.

I spoke at this same church again a few weeks later. Before the meeting started, I went with Pastor Jim and his prayer team to pray for the service. David turned to me with a smile and said, "Well, Billy, we are not going to be able to do it again today. I won't be reading the verse you will be preaching from. I am not reading a Bible verse today but will be sharing a few other things."

I laughed and said, "We'll see."

After the praise and worship and before the message, David went up to receive the offering and say a few words. He began his words with, "If we only have faith when we understand everything, we will live with a lot of doubt. There will be times *when you don't understand*." He then took the offering and sat down.

I went to the podium to bring the morning message. "Well, David," I said, "we have done it again." I then held up the first page of my notes and showed him and the congregation a phrase I had previously written in large letters and circled: "WHEN YOU DON'T UNDERSTAND." This time the Lord had led him to quote the very topic of my message.

This was one of those quiet miracles when it feels like the Lord is "giving us a special treat." I think *He* delights to reveal Himself and bless those who love and serve Him.

3

An Encouraging Word

THE PARAGRAPHS BELOW ARE NOTES FROM MY JOURNAL WRITTEN back in 2001, about eighteen years ago. They are vivid examples of how the Lord can encourage us with a word in a season when we need it most.

January 29, 2001

I was sitting at my desk preparing to go to work one morning and struggling with frustration at where I was in my life. I had gone from being a successful pastor to facing the failure of a new church plant and trying to find a job that would provide for my family. Looking through a notebook, I came upon a poem I had previously written to encourage myself to persevere and trust the Lord in the waiting process: *"When it seems you are forgotten and your good days in the past, His grace brings forth a new song. He saves the best for last."*

The poem was based on the words spoken to Jesus when He turned the water into wine: *"And he said to him, 'Every man at the beginning sets out the good wine ... and then the inferior. You have kept the good wine until now!'"* (John 2:10). Laurel and I believed this was God's plan for our life and "ministry." The best is being saved for last.

In a flash, I thought of all the good words the Lord had spoken into my heart over recent years. I realized I had to resist the temptation to be angry at my situation and resist feelings of failure and feelings of being forgotten and abandoned.

I closed my notebook and started to rise but decided to read a verse of Scripture before going to work. I reached over and opened my Bible. It fell open to Ecclesiastes 7:8–10. It was like an audible voice from God. Each word applied to me:

> The end of a thing is better than the beginning; the patient in spirit is better than the proud in spirit. Do not hasten in your spirit to be angry, for anger rests in the bosom of fools. Do not say, "Why were the former days better than these?" For you do not inquire wisely concerning this.

I knew the Lord was encouraging me to stand in faith and confidence and to trust Him for what He would yet do.

February 14, 2001

I stopped by an auto shop a couple miles from my home. As I walked out of the office and across the parking lot to my van, I was feeling the stress of financial pressure and a little despair and distress at my perplexity concerning direction for my life. I had cried out to the Lord in prayer the night before, and Laurel and I had prayed together before I left the house that morning.

As I walked across the parking lot, a black fellow in a bright red shirt who was at the other end of the building yelled to me across the parking lot, *"God will make a way! No matter what the trouble, God will make a way! Just praise Him!"* I did not know this man. I had never seen him before. But I received his word as from an angel of God, for he was truly sent to me by the Lord.

Then, like icing on the cake, the very next week, our grandson Christian, who was not more than three years old at the time, just out of the blue said to Laurel, "God will take care of you, Gammy."

I believe the Lord speaks to us on every side if we will only listen. He reveals Himself and strengthens us as we face the issues of life. That word does not remove us from the battle, but rather helps us to "fight the good fight" (1 Tim. 1:18).

> But as for me, I trust in You, O Lord; I say, "You are my God."
> My times are in Your hand. (Ps. 31:14–15)

4

Mistakes Are Part of Growth

"Hot Off the Griddle of Heaven"

PASTOR AND MRS. VARNELL DID ALL THEY COULD TO ENCOURAGE us young college "preacher boys." Their little church in a nearby town provided many opportunities for us to speak at their meetings. I remember one special occasion when Pastor Varnell called me and said, "You boys come and preach this Sunday." Usually, one of us would deliver the sermon, but on a couple occasions, we did a "tag team" message, dividing the time up between us. On this particular occasion, Pastor Varnell was letting us decide who would address his congregation.

Our circle of aspiring ministers consisted of Larry, Lonnie, Mike, George, and me. On this particular Sunday, however, Larry Rodeffer and I were the only ones able to attend the meeting. On our drive to the church, I turned to Larry and asked, "Do you have the message?" He shook his head and said, "No, Billy. I don't have a thing. Do you?" Very confidently, I replied, "Yes, Larry. I've got the message."

We arrived at the church, went in, and took our seats on the platform beside the pastor. I began looking through my Bible, doing some last-minute preparation for the sermon. Larry was sitting there, relaxed with his Bible lying on the seat beside him.

When it came time for the sermon, Pastor Varnell walked up to the podium and said, "Brother Billy and Brother Larry are with us this morning, and one of these boys has a message 'hot off the griddle of heaven.'" He turned and looked at us, and I gave the signal that I would be the one he should introduce.

I walked up to the podium, read a few verses from Luke 4, said a prayer, and then looked out at the congregation. But to my great horror, my mind went blank. I had preached from those verses many times, but this time I could not find the message. As I began to mumble to the congregation, I thought to myself, *Oh Lord God, how am I going to get out of this? I have read the scripture and said the prayer. Once you do that you are into the message. But I have nothing to say. What am I to do?*

A brilliant idea came to mind. I paused a second, and then with renewed confidence and peace, I looked at all those people and said, "You all remember what I have said—as Brother Larry brings us the message."

I then went to my seat and sat down, looking at Larry with that "innocent" guilty look on my face.

Without saying a word, Larry looked at me in a mild shock and very slowly picked up his Bible and walked over to the podium. He laid his Bible on the pulpit, opened it up, and then slowly looked back and stared at me for about three seconds with that questioning look of surprise and shock still on his face.

He then gained his composure, told the congregation to turn to the chapter where Jesus healed the woman with the issue of blood, and proceeded to give one of the best sermons he had ever given.

"Brother Larry" did have the message. I did not. And though Larry had not planned to speak at that particular moment, he drew from the resources of his life of prayer and study and gave a message that really did turn out to be "hot off the griddle of heaven," as Pastor Varnell had promised in his introduction. Larry was the only one there who knew I had been rescued from a predicament. His success overshadowed my mistake.

Mistakes are part of growth.

We must be willing to make mistakes and stumble in order to learn and grow. It takes faith to be willing to take risks. Peter spoke up and was wrong a few times but learned in the process. In the Bible, we see men of God moving in great success, accomplishment, victory, and accuracy in the things of God, yet we also see them in failure, missteps, and errors of judgment. Why is it that we have difficulty seeing ourselves on either end of this spectrum? We are shocked to think that we can experience and participate in the same successes as those men of the Bible. We also are shocked and discouraged when we find ourselves in the same types of mistakes and failures. Too often we are content to stay on some path of mediocrity and safety where we do nothing great and make no major mistakes. We even think this is where we belong. But that is not real life as God intended for us. God meant for us to learn and grow. And to do that, we need to be willing to take risks in our walk of faith.

Likewise, leaders must not be afraid of people making mistakes. Often church leadership is afraid to create an atmosphere where people can take risks, especially in the things of the Holy Spirit. They are afraid people will become strange and spooky or get into some eccentric and crazy behavior. Therefore, they prohibit people from stepping out and taking initiative. My philosophy has been that church members should have freedom to speak up and "step out" as long as they give the leadership and their brothers and sisters permission and liberty to correct and instruct them in the process. This atmosphere of freedom and love where people are comfortable attempting obedience and unafraid of failure yet loyal to truth, teachable, and willing to be corrected rather than indulged or rejected is what we see in the relationships of the twelve disciples in their walk with Jesus and each other. This same atmosphere is good for us also. Training and growth require the freedom to stumble and slip a bit.

5

Dealing with Stumbles and Failures

Peter's Examples

Jesus answered and said to him, "Blessed are you Simon Bar-Jonah, for flesh and blood has not revealed this to you, but My Father who is in heaven."

—Matthew 16:17

But He turned and said to Peter, "Get behind Me, Satan! You are an offense to Me, for you are not mindful of the things of God, but the things of men.".

—Matthew 16:23

WE LEARN THROUGH OUR MISTAKES IF WE REMAIN HUMBLE, teachable, and willing to listen. In one moment, Peter received a great revelation from the Father; the next moment, he was influenced by the enemy. In one moment, he was praised for his insight; the next moment, he was rebuked for speaking without knowledge. Experiences such as these helped Peter to grow in discernment. If Peter and the other disciples had to learn through their mistakes, how much more should we expect to do the same? Instruction and discipline are the way of life. We should not be surprised and ashamed when we need them.

Lord, let us build three tabernacles… (Luke 9:33)

Peter stood in the glory of God and, even there, spoke foolishly. He wanted to build tabernacles to Moses and Elijah. The Father had to silence him and move Peter's focus back to Jesus. It is a mistake to think a person is infallible just because he has been in the glory of God's presence. Experiencing the miraculous and the supernatural does not guarantee that a person's every thought, idea, and response is accurate. God uses imperfect vessels. Likewise, if God uses a person in one area, that does not make him perfect or an expert in other areas. Once again Peter learned from his mistakes.

Lord, bid me come. (Matt. 14:24–31)

Peter was nervous about taking the risk. Therefore, he did not say, "Let me come," walking on the water but rather, "Command me to come." The clear commission removes the fear. At His command, we can go forward in faith. And even if we, like Peter, begin to sink, we can still rejoice that we were going to Jesus in faith as opposed to staying safely in the boat with those who never fail but who never accomplish anything either.

When Peter began to sink, he did not drown in failure but called out, "Lord, save me!" God is more pleased with those who stumble while attempting to walk on water than with those who remain safely in the boat.

But I have prayed for you, that your faith should not fail; and when you have returned to Me, strengthen your brethren. (Luke 22:32)

Jesus did not rebuke Peter for the denial that was to come but rather encouraged him and prayed that he would respond properly, repent, and come through it in faith rather than giving up and quitting. Jesus wanted him to come through the situation strong and able to strengthen others.

Your ability to strengthen and encourage others does not come from your never failing, nor does it come from your always being strong but rather from your ability to break and "turn again" to repent and appropriate grace when you have failed or have sinned. Don't let faith fail when you fail.

The Lord turned and looked at Peter. (Luke 22:61)

The Lord turned and looked at Peter at the very moment Peter was denying Him. Considering the context, this is one of the most precious sentences in the Bible. The sovereignty and love of God are revealed in this glance. That look was not one of condemnation but of mercy, acceptance, and encouragement. God had providentially orchestrated the events of Jesus' trial so that Jesus would be able to turn and look at Peter at just the right moment. That glance came at the perfect time to encourage Peter and remind him of Jesus' words: "I have prayed for you that your faith should not fail; and when you have turned again, strengthen your brethren."

...What diligence it [godly sorrow] produced in you...
(2 Cor. 7:11)

What will you do with your shame? Just be embarrassed or be broken and turn to the Lord?

Often people are humiliated but not humbled. We must find godly sorrow and not the "sorrow of the world." Worldly sorrow can be a form of self-centeredness and rebellion. It causes us to wallow in self-pity, to remain in the pit, and to stay stubborn before God. Godly sorrow causes us to arise, to depend upon God's mercy, and to appropriate His transforming and enabling grace.

6

Dealing with Regrets

LOOK BACK OVER MY LIFE AND SEE MANY REGRETS, THINGS I would change or do better if I could go back and start over. I see areas where I was not a wise and faithful steward of resources, time, responsibilities, opportunities, and potential. How do I resolve what in the natural seems to be unresolvable? What do I do when I've lost or forfeited something I can never get back? How do I find comfort when something dear to me is gone? The answer: I give it to God.

The prodigal son left home and wasted his inheritance in the world of disobedience and sin. Sometimes I feel like the prodigal who stayed home. I did not waste my life in sin and dissipation but rather was the "good son" who stayed in the fold but still squandered opportunities, resources, time, and potential. This brings deep and painful regret that feels like it comes when it might be too late to recover or redeem the situation.

Based on the prophet Nathan's word to him, David knew his own sin with Bathsheba and the death of her husband were partly responsible for Absalom's death and the rebellion that had entered his household. His grief was almost unimaginable. We see David's heart-wrenching cry upon learning of Absalom's death.

> The king was deeply moved, and went up to the chamber over the gate, and wept. And as he went, he said thus: "O my son Absalom, my son, my son!" (2 Sam. 18:33)

> The king covered his face, and cried out with a loud voice, "O my son Absalom! O Absalom, my son, my son.!" (2 Sam. 19:4)

Most of us have some regrets regarding our performance as parents. As a father, I have prayed many times for the Lord to deliver my children from the consequences of my failures. So many blind spots I have come to see when it feels too late to do anything about it. I have asked for my children's forgiveness. And I turn to prayer and God's Word. I have found and clung to those Scripture verses that promise God's redemptive and saving power over children. Of course, there are many other areas where we have regrets. The same principles apply.

Looking back over my pastoral ministry, I have also prayed for the Lord to bless and heal anyone I may have unintentionally hurt, wounded, or misled. It is common to man. Everyone makes mistakes. None of us walks with absolute perfection. We all have things we regret. And there are the blind spots that are still hidden and leaving damage in our wake. We ask the Lord to show us. The wicked and selfish person has no regrets and no grief. It is the more spiritual person who bows in repentance and weeps over his sins. It is the more faithful and honest person who cries out, "Oh wretched man that I am! Who will deliver me from this body of death?"

So, what do I do as I look back seeing these areas of loss and so many things I would change? I ask for mercy and forgiveness, and I ask Him to bless everyone I may have hurt, wounded, or failed in any way. I receive His mercy and restoration with great thanksgiving, but also, I surrender and submit to the Lord's loving discipline in my life ... whatever that may entail. Whether restoration or forfeiture, this requires great faith and trust in God, His goodness, and His wisdom.

So, what do I do as I look back, seeing these areas of loss and so many things I would change? I give it to God. My hope is in the redemptive power of Jesus Christ and in the grace, wisdom, and goodness of God that helps me overcome myself.

> Nevertheless I am not ashamed, for I know whom I have believed and am persuaded that He is able to keep what I have committed to Him until that Day. (2 Tim. 1:12)

I give it to God after I have given myself to Him.

7

Did I "Miss It"?

I N OUR DARKEST MOMENTS, WE OFTEN THINK WE HAVE FAILED OR
that we have not lived up to our potential. To some degree, this may be
true for most of us. But ultimately, we must do our best ... and leave the
judgment to God.

In a dark dungeon and about to be beheaded, John the Baptist sent
word to Jesus, saying, "Are you the Coming One, or do we look for another?" (Matt. 11:3). These sad words express the despair of one who, for a
moment, thought he had failed. Jesus responded with words of reassur-
ance, letting John know that the work he started was going forth gloriously
with signs and wonders and that John had correctly pointed to Jesus as the
Lamb of God sent to take away the sins of the world.

A Friend's Question

A friend who was struggling with a sense of failure recently sent me the
following message:

> Here is my question, Billy Long: If I can't see that I have ac-
> complished much with my life thus far for the kingdom, and
> certainly not what I may have expected to back in our salad
> days at ORU, how realistic is it to believe my story is going to
> dramatically alter and start counting for something at sixty
> years old?! (And don't even get me to speculate as to whether
> I would be willing to endure anything like what R____ has in
> order for that dramatic change to occur.) —L. P.

My Response

We must serve Jesus Christ in the present. Obedience now (today) is not based on what we accomplished *yesterday*. We walk with Him NOW. Tomorrow is in His hands. The fruit and the results are also all in His hands. I don't obey and walk with Him today based on what I think I will have accomplished tomorrow. I don't obey today based on whether or not I did yesterday. I reach out and take His hand today and follow Him *now*.

Fruit and accomplishments are also His to judge and deal with. Pick any Israelite family during the 400 years in Egypt when God was silent, and all they knew was the routine daily trudge and toil as slaves. Subjectively, it would have felt like the biggest waste and futility of life. But they *had* to just *be there*. Even when empty, desperate, half-dead, and hurting, they had to just simply be a link in the lineage, a holder of the baton until the fullness of time came and Moses arrived to take them to Canaan. There had to be physical lineage links from Jacob and Joseph to Moses and Canaan.

God is the judge of success and failure.

David completed his course and served the purpose of God in his generation (Acts 13:36) even though his life was not perfect. There were many incidences in his life in which he could have been called a failure, yet he still went on to fulfill God's purpose and was called a man after God's heart. David's example shows us that God, while not condoning sin and irresponsibility, does factor in our mistakes, failures, and shortcomings. He probably makes more allowances for these things than we do. "For He knows our frame; He remembers that we are dust" (Ps. 103:14). Therefore, He extends great mercy and abundant grace to those who sincerely desire and seek to do His will.

There are examples in the Bible of people who genuinely failed in God's service, but generally these failures are indicative of heart problems rather than competency issues. King Saul is an example. He was disqualified and removed from the throne, not because he lacked skill at being a king, but because he did not have a heart to obey the Lord (Acts 13:22; 1 Cor. 9:27). He failed in his obedience and faith, and he refused to surrender to the will of God. The issue comes back to the heart. A person who is rebellious at heart will fail and then use his failure as an excuse to further disobey. A person who has a heart after God may stumble but will get back up and persevere in his attempt to please God and do His will.

God is the ultimate judge of success and failure. In one phase of ministry, I felt I was riding a graceful and beautiful thoroughbred. In another phase, I felt I was riding a bucking bronco, tossed and thrown. A third situation felt like sitting on an old sway-back, gray mule who could barely stand up. The first seemed a success, the second a partial success and a partial failure, while the third started off slow and then gradually tapered off—basically, it failed. But things are not always as they seem. Man and God do not always esteem things the same, and the mysteries of His will are not always known to us. Therefore, in all circumstances, we should endure and hold to Jesus in faith. We should do our best and let God be the judge. Sometimes we succeed in God's plan while failing in our own, while at other times we fail in our own while succeeding in His. What we think is failure may not be failure at all. But when the failure is real, God is able to work redemptively and turn our shame into double honor.

Let me not be ashamed, for I put my trust in You. (Ps. 25:20)

8

He Would Have Passed Them By?

Immediately He made His disciples get into the boat and go before Him to the other side...Then He saw them straining at rowing, for the wind was against them. Now about the fourth watch of the night He came to them, walking on the sea, and would have passed them by.

—Mark 6:45, 48

THIS CHAPTER HAS MANY ENCOURAGING INSIGHTS. IT DEALS WITH *the significance of a "boat" and how we should face the "storm" when it seems the Lord has sent us on ahead without Him and when it feels like the Lord is passing us by.*

"He made His disciples get into a boat."

The "boat" is significant because it represents a context from which we cannot easily escape. The disciples, on that small boat in the middle of the sea, could not simply change their minds and walk away from the problems and issues at hand. They could not escape the process; they had to ride it out.

The Lord desires to work deeply and significantly in our lives, but He knows that human nature wants to run from the fire and will attempt to escape if it has the option to do so. We would rather sin than suffer, and in the crunch, we seek relief rather than the purpose and glory of God. We tend to be like the psalmist who cried out,

> So I said, "Oh, that I had wings like a dove! I would fly away and be at rest. Indeed, I would wander far off, and remain in the wilderness. I would hasten my escape from the windy storm and tempest." (Ps. 55:6–8)

It is interesting to note that a "successful" escape leads only to "wandering" and to "the wilderness." Wandering gives the illusion of freedom, and the wilderness gives the temporary illusion of comfort, only because it is less intense than the crucible God designed for our change and growth.

This explains the boat. He places us in a classroom or training context from which we cannot escape, bypass, or take the easy way out, at least not with integrity and righteousness. This is a good thing. It shows that God loves us enough to work with us in spite of ourselves.

"He made … His disciples go before Him."

Jesus promises to go "before His sheep" when He sends them forth, but here He commands His disciples to go "before Him." This seems to be in contrast to the promise, and when it happens to us, we are tempted to feel alone and left to ourselves.

But the reality is the opposite. The psalmist, in his dark hour, feeling forgotten and forsaken and crying out daily with sorrow in his heart, came to understand that God was actually dealing bountifully with him. Sometimes our darkest moments indicate God's most intense presence rather than His absence. We must remember that the disciples, although in the middle of the sea in a storm at night, were not really alone. Miles away and through the darkness, "Jesus saw them." With Him, there is no darkness nor distance. God may be out of our sight, but we are never out of His sight. He saw them and went straight to them. They were not ignored by God. On the contrary, the whole experience had been designed especially for them. They were getting special attention. As one story goes, we see only one set of footprints not because He is not walking with us but because He is carrying us.

"He ... would have passed them by."

This sentence requires more discussion than can be done in this short space. It represents a principle that Christians often miss. While there is such a thing as divine resistance which is accompanied by the absence of grace, there is also an area in our training where we encounter what appears to be divine resistance but which is actually the Lord's desire to stimulate us to aggressive faith and prayer, to provoke us out of passivity and apathy, and to move us to the assertive and determined action of obedient children passionate to do His will. It is a place where we work together with Him through intercession and patient endurance. How often do we let the Lord pass on by because we think that is what He wants to do? How often do we interpret His apparent reluctance as a genuine lack of interest? We think He does not want to engage us, and so we back away, drop the subject, and let Him pass on by. It is clear that Jesus never intended to pass by that boat. His heart was with those men. They were the object of His special care and focus at that moment. We should take note and learn from this example.

There are other biblical examples of God's children pressing into Him when on the surface it appeared they were encountering resistance. The two men on the road to Emmaus constrained Jesus to stay with them when He made as though He would have left them behind and gone on further. The Canaanite woman cried out to Jesus and obtained healing for her daughter after Jesus had given her three negative (almost offensive) responses (that would have caused most of us to turn and walk away). In wrestling with the Angel of the Lord, Jacob said, "I will not let You go unless You bless me!" (Gen. 32:26).

I don't fully understand this principle, but I do know that God wants us to "trouble" Him with things. Our quickness to let Him pass on by is not courtesy, but rather complacency, passivity, and spiritual laziness. Sometimes it reflects our low self-esteem. We think we are not worthy of His attention and help. But ultimately, it reflects our lack of understanding of God's love and desire to be involved in our lives.

"He made His disciples ... go ... to the other side."

Our destiny is the "other side," which means we will make it through. We must not be afraid of the storm that comes on the way. Jesus will silence and still it as soon as its purpose is completed. The experience in the boat was to make them grow and to cause them to know Him at a deeper level. Peter even had the opportunity to walk on the water with Jesus at this time. So maybe our goal should be not simply to get to the other side, but to be at His side. Let's not jump to the conclusion that the Lord does not want to be bothered, that He has better things to do. Let's touch the hem of His garment and cry out to Him to abide with us. Let's also cry out to Him as Peter did: "Lord, if it is you, command me to come to you on the water" (Mark 14:28). We will find that He is not only present, but very present, "a very present help in trouble." (Ps. 46:1).

Biblical references for further study: Mark 6:45–52; John 10:3–5; Luke 24:28; Matt.15:21–28; Gen. 32:22–32; Luke 11:5–8; Luke 18:1–5; Ps. 13; Matt. 14:22–32; Heb. 10:19–23; Ps. 46:1.

9

The Struggle to Find Comfort

In the multitude of my anxieties within me, Your comforts delight my soul.

— Psalm 94:19.

THE LAST TWO YEARS HAVE SEEN MORE DEATHS AND SORROW than any other time I can remember. Therefore, I thought it would be good to share this message on comfort. This message will be beneficial to those who have suffered loss. Sometimes we need to be reminded that the Lord is not only present, but He is a "very present" help in time of need.

Refusing Comfort

Then Jacob tore his clothes, put sackcloth on his waist, and mourned for his son many days. And all his sons and all his daughters arose to comfort him; but he refused to be comforted, and he said, "For I shall go down into the grave to my son in mourning." Thus his father wept for him.

—Genesis 37:34–35

"Refusing comfort" refers to the state in which the loss or pain is so great and final that there seems to be absolutely nothing that could possibly heal the hurt, relieve the pain, or replace the loss. Jacob found himself in this condition as he experienced heart-wrenching grief over the loss of his son Joseph. No one was able to comfort him. No words could relieve or console him.

Genuine, Not Superficial

To a person in such grief, the idea of comfort often seems like an empty and futile promise. Consolation is viewed much like the consolation prize which is usually given to the losers of a contest. The "consolation game" is a contest for those who have lost early in the tournament. Likewise, a person in the intensity of his pain often tends to view attempts at comfort as being merely the "consolation game" or the "consolation prize," a substitute for the real thing, a shallow and superficial attempt to make him feel better.

This, however, is not what the Bible means by "comfort." God's comfort is real and genuine, not imaginary or illusory. It is supernatural and comes from and with God Himself. There is a depth of reality and glory and a supernatural quality in genuine comfort which makes it substantial. It represents real healing rather than a mere superficial "second prize."

In God Himself

Job could find no comfort in words, rationalizations, or in sweet thoughts from friends. He, like Jacob, found that there are times when the anguish, the loss, the disappointment, and the hurt are so great that nothing will comfort because nothing can change what has happened. He also discovered that it is difficult to find comfort in the midst of so many unanswered questions when there is suffering without explanation and understanding. The great question "Why?" sometimes stands between us and our comfort.

In these times, our comfort, relief, and hope are in God Himself, not in ideas, words, or in anything that could be said. Our comfort comes only in God, in the revelation of His presence, in seeing Him and His eternal perspective. He comes to us Himself and brings a comfort that is supernatural and beyond comprehension. It is interesting to note that Job, with the confusion and questions that must have been swirling around in his head, posed none of them to God during the divine visitation. Seeing the Lord brought a supernatural revelation and understanding that needed no further explanation.

God's visit makes the difference.

Before God visited Job, no one could comfort him for the loss of his children and reputation. No one could soothe the pain of his boils nor answer any of his questions. But all of this was resolved when God came to him. Job arose in joy and relief as he looked into the eyes of the Eternal. Any questions he may have had were answered in the supernatural touch and in the revelation of God Himself. Once Job resolved his situation between himself and God, he was then able to receive comfort from and be comforted by his friends.

From Job and Jacob, we learn that comfort does not usually come instantly but rather follows certain processes such as the normal time needed for grief, as well as the time required to take care of necessary spiritual transactions between us and God. We need to realize that God loves us, that He desires to reveal Himself to us and bring us into His presence to receive enabling power by His grace. He may come to us in our private prayers, or He may reach out to us through the love and touch of a friend or through fellow Christians. He may allow us to grieve for a while, but He will not leave us bereaved and desolate. He has sent the Holy Spirit to be His Presence with us to strengthen, encourage, and comfort (John 14:16–18).

> ...It was too painful for me—until I went into the sanctuary...
> (Ps. 73:16–17)

> I have heard of you by the hearing of the ear, but now my eyes see you. (Job 42:5)

> ...in Your presence is fullness of joy; at your right hand are pleasures forevermore. (Ps. 16:11)

> Blessed be the God and Father of our Lord Jesus Christ, the Father of mercies and God of all comfort, who comforts us in all our tribulation... (2 Cor. 1:3–4)

10

Facing Eternity

I WROTE THIS CHAPTER TO ENCOURAGE CHRISTIANS TO BE AT PEACE knowing that beyond the veil of this flesh, there is a glorious and wonderful eternity awaiting us.

My second purpose is to awaken the unbeliever to the realities of the spiritual realm and to fact that each person must face eternity and give an account to God.

Raised from the Dead

The spiritual realm is real. There are many people, including some friends of mine, whose experiences prove there is more to life than what we see with our eyes and touch with our physical senses. I am sharing some of these testimonies in the paragraphs below.

H. A. Baker was a missionary to China from 1919 to 1950. In his book *Visions Beyond the Veil*, he tells of an outpouring of the Holy Spirit that fell upon the children of his mission's orphanage in China. The children saw visions of heaven, hell, demons, and angels. I recently read the book *Heaven Is for Real*, written by a pastor about the experiences of his pre-school son who was taken to heaven and back during a surgery in which the child almost died. The testimonies in these books are amazing.

I have an acquaintance in Charleston, South Carolina, who was struck by lightning in his yard and was technically dead. His spirit left his body and was lifted into the air above his house. From there, he looked down and saw his body being placed into an EMS vehicle and his wife standing in the yard, asking the Lord not to take her husband. He saw heaven, Jesus, and family members who were there. He was overwhelmed by the beauty, peace, love, and wonders of it all and did not want to leave. Jesus told him he had to return, and suddenly, he was back in his body. He tells how he was depressed at first for having to come back but then realized he needed to rejoice and share his wonderful testimony.

I have a friend in California named Marvin Ford who died of a heart attack and lay in the hospital dead for thirty minutes. His spirit left his body, and from above, he could see the doctor and people gathered around his body. He was suddenly in the presence of the Lord and saw the over-whelming and inexpressible beauty of heaven. The Lord showed him many things during that visit. Then he looked down and saw his pastor entering the hospital to pray for God to raise him up. "Uh oh, Lord," he said. "Here comes trouble." He knew he had to return but did not want to. Neverthe-less, the pastor prayed, and God sent Marvin back. This was the beginning of a preaching ministry that has taken him around the world.

I had a professor in college who died and was raised from the dead when prayed for by this same pastor.

A Near-Death Experience During Surgery

Below are excerpts from a letter sent to me my by good friend Ashur Cordes from Minnesota. He tells of his near-death experience that occurred during surgery in which the doctors did not expect him to survive. A Christian nurse on duty told the family, "The only thing that will save him now is prayer." So the family went into the intensive care area and prayed. They called on friends around the world to pray. Then Ashur had a miracle. His spirit left his body, and he saw the Lord right there with him, and he saw heaven in the distance.

He was so amazed that the Lord was right there like a brother hug-ging him and healing him. Feeling he did not deserve to be in the Lord's presence, he asked, "What about my sins?' The Lord's response was, "I took care of that on the cross." The answer was explained by John 3:16: "For God so loved the world that He gave His only begotten Son, that whoever believes in Him should not perish but have everlasting life."

Ashur then saw what appeared to be a stream of crystal clear water flowing from the Lord to his body along with a golden light that sur-rounded his bed. Suddenly, he was healed.

There are medical records that verify and confirm his condition and recovery.

Ashur later spoke with a Christian friend in Fargo who was not at the hospital but who had prayed in his home about ten miles away. Ashur, in his vision, actually heard his friend praying and a week later was able to quote the prayer back to his friend word for word. He also heard the prayers of others around the world praying for him. He describes it this way: "I was very aware of prayers flooding in for me. I heard those prayers. Then I heard the Lord's order that the prayers be answered. And those prayers were in His mighty and kind hands, and *He* directed them into my heart while I watched from eight feet above my bed. I was healed."

"It did not feel like death."

Lonnie, another one of my Christian friends, was in a hospital bed and close to death. He could feel himself slipping away and knew he was one moment away from eternity. God's incomprehensible love and inexpressible peace were so real that he actually wanted to go on and be with the Lord. He very profoundly described his experience in this way: "It did not feel like death." He experienced the reality of the Apostle Paul's word that death has lost its sting and the grave has lost its victory ... and that victory is through the death and resurrection of Jesus Christ.

The thing that shone brightest to my friends who came so close to death was the incomprehensible greatness of God's love and the awesome efficacy of the blood of Jesus and the cross of Christ. God really loves us and wants us to be at peace in Him.

Why take the risk?

It is very sad to be "without hope and without God in the world," (Eph. 2:12 NIV), but it is even more grievous to face an everlasting eternity without the Lord. There are many who do not believe in God, and they assume that death is the end and everyone at death enters some sort of oblivion. There can be no comfort or peace in this ideology since, if true, it would mean the eternal loss of all we love, and it gives no hope for anything beyond this current life, which is so short and in itself holds so much suffering.

There are also those who believe there is a God, but who do not aggressively seek to know Him. They take the risk that God grades on the curve. They think, "I have been a good person. My good outweighs my bad, and so I'll make it into heaven because I am a good person." The problem with this is that the Scripture makes it very clear we are not saved by our works or our own righteousness, but only by the death and resurrection of Jesus Christ and by His grace (unmerited favor) and by faith rather than good works. The problem with the "I am a good person" approach is that it leaves a person unsure and simply not really knowing and with no real peace. The person who makes a firm commitment to Jesus Christ as Lord is the one who faces death with true peace, hope, and certainty.

Live in Peace, Rest in Peace

Will Durant, in his volumes on world history, gives a vivid account of the difference between the pagan Romans and the persecuted Christians of that era. It was said of Christians that their lives consisted of persecutions above ground and prayers below ground. Here are some very profound quotes from Durant:

> In the catacombs below Rome, Christian graves tell the terrible tale. Heads were found severed from the body, ribs and shoulder blades broken, and bones often calcined from fire … But despite the awful story of persecution, note the inscriptions on the Christians' graves.
>
> "Here lies Marcia, put to rest in a dream of peace."
>
> "Lawrence to his sweetest son, borne away of angels."
>
> "Victorious in peace and in Christ."
>
> "Being called away, he went in peace."

Pagan Epitaphs

Durant also shows us how the pagan epitaphs of the Romans stand in stark contrast to those of the Christians:

> "Live for the present hour, since we are sure of nothing else."

"I lift my hands against the gods who took me away at the age of 20 though I had done no harm."

"Once I was not. Now I am not. I know nothing about it."

"Traveler, curse me not as you pass, for I am in darkness and cannot answer."

Our Assurance in Christ

It is a fearful thing to face eternity without God. Knowing these spiritual realities, we should cry out to God to know Him and serve Him and to intercede for our loved ones. I pray daily for my family, friends, and others on my prayer list. I cry to God for their salvation and for them to know Jesus Christ our Lord and Savior. The greatest grief for me would be to stand by the coffin of a loved one without full assurance of his or her relationship with Jesus.

> Therefore, having been justified by faith, we have peace with God through our Lord Jesus Christ, through whom also we have access by faith into this grace in which we stand, and rejoice in hope of the glory of God. (Rom. 5:1–2)

> ...lay hold of the hope set before us. This hope we have as an anchor of the soul, both sure and steadfast, and which enters the Presence behind the veil, where the forerunner [Christ] has entered for us... (Heb. 6:18–20)

11

In Whose Hands?

*For ... You have known my soul in adversities, and have not shut
me up into the hand of the enemy.*

—Psalm 31:7–8

THE FOLLOWING PARAGRAPHS ARE INTENDED TO HELP US SEE THAT
*God's hand is the undergirding "moving sidewalk" that is constantly carrying us forward in His purpose, even when the enemy and circumstances try
to pull us in the opposite direction. Lawless hands may "grab" us, but God's hand
rules. We must see ourselves in God's hands rather than victims of those who mistreat us.*

Whose Prisoner?

...I, Paul, the prisoner of Christ Jesus for you...

—Ephesians 3:1

*Therefore do not be ashamed of the testimony of our Lord, nor of me
His prisoner....*

—2 Timothy 1:8

The Apostle Paul did not take on the role of victim nor did he rail against those who placed him in chains. Focusing upon them would have depleted his spiritual life, leaving him bitter and frustrated. He counted himself a "prisoner of the Lord," not of the Romans. And his enemies, without realizing it, sent him to the very city (Rome) to which Jesus had told him to go (Acts 23:11). His epistles from the Roman prison are in our Bible today and have been read by millions. Though he was bound, the Word of God was not bound. His testimony is a poignant reminder that we are in the hands of God, not in the hands of those who afflict us.

Who Sent Joseph?

And the patriarchs, becoming envious, sold Joseph into Egypt. But God was with him.

—Acts 7:9

He [God] sent a man before them—Joseph— who was sold as a slave.

—Psalm 105:17

Joseph's brothers sold him to traders who carried him off to Egypt in chains where he served as a slave and was unjustly accused and imprisoned. His "owners" and masters controlled all the decisions for his life. They hurt him and had no regard for his God, yet they unwittingly sent him to the very position of which God had spoken in the prophetic dreams of Joseph's youth.

"God sent me."

But now, do not therefore be grieved or angry with yourselves because you sold me here; for God sent me before you to preserve life.

—Genesis 45:5

Had Joseph focused on the cruel acts of his brothers and masters, he would have developed the victim mentality with all its self-centeredness, ungodly attitudes, and deficiencies of character. He would have been overwhelmed with bitterness and anger. He might have written a book with a sad ending about how he had been mistreated and sent to Egypt as a slave. He most likely would have committed adultery with Potiphar's wife and wasted away in prison.

Joseph, however, did not focus on those who mistreated him. His business and call were higher. On the surface, it appeared that his brothers in cruelty had sent him to Egypt, but the truth is that God sent him to save his family and a nation and to settle his people in a place where they could grow and develop until God was ready for them to enter the promised land 400 years later. Lawless hands had "grabbed" him, but God's hand ruled.

In Whose Hands?

> *Him, being delivered over by the determined purpose and fore-knowledge of God, you have taken by lawless hands, have crucified, and put to death; whom God raised up, having loosed the pains of death, because it was not possible that He should be held by it.*

> —Acts 2:23–24

"Lawless hands" were at work with malevolent intent grabbing Jesus to crucify Him upon a cross, and yet beneath it all was the hand of God delivering Jesus over to His determined purpose. Here is the mystery of God's sovereignty. The actions of wicked men against an innocent person were turned to the purpose of God and to the salvation of the world.

Oppressed people tend to see only the "lawless hands" that mistreat them. The result is loss of faith accompanied by harmful and ungodly attitudes. Jesus, however, kept His heart toward the Father's plan, knowing that the redemptive hand of God was at work to fulfill the greater purpose of God. The enemy's plan backfired. Christ became the crucified lamb of God that takes away the sins of the world, and He was raised from the dead as our Lord and Savior.

We are in the hands of God.

The sovereign hand of God undergirds and holds us in spite of the "lawless hands" that work against us. His hand is the "moving sidewalk" on which we stand and which carries us forward even when it seems the enemy and life attempt to carry us backwards.

When we spend our emotional, mental, and spiritual energy on the "brothers" who "threw us into the pit" or the "Romans" who "threw us into prison," we make ourselves their victims and their prisoners. But when we engage the Lord, surrender to Him, and stand in faith with a right spirit, we experience the grace and power of God working all things together for our good and to His purpose.

We may not always be given the most comfortable route. The Apostle Paul might have preferred to go to Rome on a wonderful Mediterranean cruise ship with the bountiful buffet meals and lively entertainment. Joseph may have preferred to go to Egypt as part of a family vacation, a group tour of the Holy Land with all the first-class accommodations and helpful tour guides, followed by a first-class excursion to Cairo. But each man's journey was painful and in chains. They took the way of the cross and drank the cup of suffering on their way to the joy set before them and to the fulfillment of a purpose which was greater than themselves and their comfort.

> When Joseph's brothers saw that their father was dead, they said, "Perhaps Joseph will hate us, and may actually repay us for all the evil which we did to him." So they sent messengers to Joseph, saying """...I beg you, please forgive the trespass of your brothers and their sin; for they did evil to you."' Now please, forgive the trespass of the servants of the God of your fathers." And Joseph wept when they spoke to him.
>
> Then his brothers also went and fell down before his face, and they said, "Behold, we are your servants."
> Joseph said to them, "Do not be afraid... But as for you, you meant evil against me; but God meant it for good, in order to bring it about as it is this day, to save many people alive..." And he comforted them and spoke kindly to them.
> (Gen. 50:15–21)

12

Misinterpreting God's Special Attention

To Esau I gave the mountains of Seir to possess, but Jacob and his children went down to Egypt.

—Joshua 24:4

I F YOU WERE ESAU, YOU MIGHT THINK GOD LOVED YOU MORE SINCE you were moving "up" the mountain (to your inheritance). If you were Jacob, you might question why God was sending you "down" to Egypt (suffering, waiting, and hardship) rather than directly to your inheritance. The truth is the Lord was not pleased with Esau, and the Lord had a special plan for Jacob (Israel) and his descendants. That special plan required special attention and preparation. We often misinterpret God's special attention and preparation in our lives.

I was observing a roofing crew at work on a phone company facility that houses equipment that runs the phone system for the surrounding region. Because of the crucial nature of the equipment in this facility and the absolute need to ensure no interruption of the phone service to customers, the contractor was required to have a man (the "spotter") stand inside and inspect the ceiling underneath the roofing work area during the early morning tear-off phase of the work. The spotter's job is to make sure there are no leaks, dust, or particles falling from the ceiling onto the equipment. His job, though very important, is relatively easy and comfortable compared to the physical labor of the men at work on the roof. Company policy requires the spotter to remain inside only during early morning tear-off and during removal of the old roofing membrane. He returns to work on the roof with the other men as soon as the tear-off phase is completed and installation of the new membrane has begun.

On this particular job, however, the foreman kept the spotter inside the building through the entire workday. The other workers complained, thinking that they were being treated unfairly and that the foreman was showing favoritism. "Why does he allow the spotter to sit inside all day while we have to work, sweat, and suffer up here in the heat? Why does he not make the spotter come back onto the roof when tear-off is completed, instead of remaining inside when it is not necessary for him to be there?"

Hearing their complaints, I went to the foreman and asked him, "Why do you allow the spotter to remain inside all day?" His response surprised me. "I don't like him. He is lazy and he doesn't do good work. I keep him down there because I don't want him around me, and I don't want him up here where the work is going on."

His response showed me how badly the working crew had misinterpreted the foreman's actions and motives. They had completely misjudged him and his opinion of them and of the spotter. He was not honoring the man who was left in the shade, and he was not disrespecting the ones who were required to work in the hot sun. On the contrary, it was his respect for their skill and diligence that caused him to keep them in the more difficult and necessary place. He needed them on the roof because he could depend on them to do a good job. It was his displeasure with the spotter that caused him to leave that worker inside in the "easier" place all day. He placed more responsibility and asked more of those from whom he expected more.

We should see in this true story a lesson in how God deals with us. Our load may represent God's pleasure and confidence in us. He requires more from those He favors. It is an honor for God to ask of you more than He asks of others. God asks more from those to whom He has given more, from whom He expects more, and upon whom He has placed a high calling.

The early Christians did not complain and say, "Why me?" during persecution and beatings for Christ's sake, but rather rejoiced that they were counted worthy to suffer for His sake. The Lord was honoring them as those "worthy to drink the cup" (Mark 10:35–39). They are the spiritual giants, not those who seem to glide along effortlessly in flowery beds of ease on a warm and balmy day. It is not a compliment when God asks nothing of you. The horses who submit to the training bridle are the ones who are chosen to pull the kings carriage, not the ones who are left to run wild and free in the pasture.

In our walk with God, we need to remember the following spiritual paradoxes. First, God often speaks louder in His silence and does greater things during what seems to be His absence. In the Father's silence as Jesus hung on the cross, Jesus cried, "Why have You forsaken Me?" Yet in that moment, God wrought salvation for the world and through it elevated Jesus to a throne of great glory. When it feels like He has forgotten us and has left us, He may actually be dealing bountifully with us (Ps. 13). His asking hard things of us and requiring more of us than seems fair may be a reflection of the high calling He has placed on us, the special attention He is giving us, and the great expectation He has regarding our character and potential.

David thought God had forgotten him but then realized the Lord had been paying special attention to him.

> How long, Lord? Will you forget me forever? How long will You hide Your face from me? (Ps. 13:1)

> I will sing to the Lord, because He has dealt bountifully with me. (Ps. 13:6)

13

He Will Not Say, "Hey, You."

A Fellow at the Mall.

YEARS AGO, WHILE STROLLING THROUGH A MALL IN DURHAM, North Carolina, I saw a mall maintenance worker who resembled my mother's cousins. In his stature, the texture of his hair, and his facial expressions, he looked exactly like them. I did not approach him at that time. But a few days later, I saw this same gentleman in the mall parking lot.

I went up to him and said, "Excuse me, sir, but you so closely resemble my mother's family down in South Carolina. Do you have any relatives in Horry County near Myrtle Beach, South Carolina." The gentleman looked at me and with a thick accent responded, "No, Señor. I don' theeenk so." He was from South America.

A Lady at the Doctor's Office

I was at my doctor's office a few days ago and saw a lady standing in the waiting area and talking with a couple other ladies. I said to myself, *Oh, look! It's Judy Johnson.* It had been a long time since I had seen her. As I walked toward her, I smiled and pointed at her and said, "Judy, is that you?" She smiled back and said, "It's good to see you," as I gave her a big hug.

It was then that I realized that this woman was a perfect stranger. I kept going and walked on past.

Getting on a Plane

I was talking with people as I waited at the gate to board an airplane. I saw a fellow who looked familiar. I asked him if we had met before. He was a stranger and said he did know me. This happens to me a lot. I'll see people who look familiar and wonder if I have met them in the past. Sometimes I'll approach and ask them.

I tend to overdo this practice.

I missed an opportunity to speak to a friend once when I was visiting Statesboro, Georgia, many years ago. I saw a young lady in a convenience store who looked like Sue Stabler, a girl I knew in high school back in South Carolina. I was bashful and did not approach her. Then a couple weeks later, I was back in South Carolina, and I ran into Sue on the street and discovered that the lady in the convenience store in Georgia was actually her. Therefore, I tend to ask people if I know them rather than risk missing out on an opportunity to visit with an old friend. That's why I was being bold at the airport.

Back at the Airport

The plane was a small commuter flight with only a few people on the plane, which made folks more comfortable and freer to interact and talk. At some point during the flight, the fellow in the seat in front of me abruptly turned around and glared at me and said, "*I am offended!*" In shock, I replied, "Why?" He then said, "I'm the only person on this plane that you have never met before."

The Friend in Atlanta

Passing through Atlanta, Gorgia, I decided to call an old friend to say hello. His wife, whom I had never met before, answered the phone. I introduced myself and said, "I'm calling to speak to Van. This is Billy Long, and I just wanted to say hello as I passed through town." She apologized, saying Van was not home and that it's been such a long time since we had spoken and she knew he would love to see me again. At some point in the conversation, I asked her how their pastor John Duke was doing. She answered that she did not know pastor John or any of the other mutual friends I named. So it turned out that after a five minute conversation, I realized I had called the wrong Van. His wife thought I was her husband's old college friend who also was named Billy.

No Mistaken Identity

In His infinite greatness, our God knows us individually. There is not and never will be any mistaken identity in God's dealing in our lives. No one will be lost in the crowd. He knows the "all," and He knows the "each." Each of us is special in His eyes. We are not on an assembly line. We are not made in a mold. He knew us before we were born and has kept up with us since birth. The psalmist says His eyes saw my substance, being yet unformed. And in His book the days fashioned for me were written when as yet there were none of them (Ps. 139:16).

He knows me. He knows you.

> ...the solid foundation of God stands, having this seal: "The Lord knows those who are His"... (2 Tim. 2:19)

> I am the good shepherd; and I know My sheep, and am known by My own. (John 10:14)

> My sheep hear My voice, and I know them, and they follow Me. (John 10:27)

You are unique in God's eyes, and He knows you and everything about you. To us who know and love Jesus, He says, "To him who overcomes I will give some of the hidden manna to eat. And I will give him a white stone, and on the stone a new name written which no one knows except him who receives it" (Rev. 2:17).

This tells me that you and I are not lost in the crowd. He knows each of us personally. Each of us is special in His eyes. Jesus said that each child has an angel who always beholds the face of the Father in heaven. What a wonderful God! What a wonderful Lord and Savior! He will call me by my name. He will not say, "Hey, you."

14

Holy, but Not Silent

SOME OF THE MOST AMAZING GLIMPSES INTO THE SPIRITUAL REALM and manifestations of God's intimate involvement with His people are seen in the Christmas story. The angel Gabriel appeared to Zacharias (father of John the Baptist), to Joseph, and to Mary. The heavens opened, causing shepherds to tremble as they saw and heard a multitude of angels praising God with a roar equivalent to Niagara Falls. John the Baptist's mother, Elizabeth, conceived him in her old age. Jesus was supernaturally placed in Mary's womb by the Holy Spirit. Joseph and Mary were led by angelic visitations and by the Holy Spirit to go to Egypt and were told when to return to Nazareth.

These and other amazing and marvelous things happened around the birth of Jesus. But the yearly and routine presentation of those experiences in church Christmas plays and manger scenes has tended to inoculate Christians to the reality and awesomeness of what actually happened. The Bible verses describing the events are usually relegated to the Christmas season and are treated as out of place during the rest of the year. We tend to envision people wearing costumes at the holiday manger scene in the church Christmas play rather than recalling the reality and awesomeness of the glorious realities experienced by those who lived it over 2,000 years ago.

The night was holy, but it was not silent. It was not a church Christmas play; it was a drama of intense proportions. Voices were heard in the full range of emotions. There were praises, prayers, weeping, grief, and joy. We should not be oblivious to the spiritual warfare and struggles that accompanied the event. How difficult it must have been for Mary to explain her "out of wedlock" condition in a culture where it was frowned upon. What grief, pain, and perplexity must have overwhelmed the weeping mothers in Bethlehem when Herod slew their innocent babies.

There is peace and joy when we know the Lord and walk with Him. But when heaven lifts the veil, reveals itself, and interacts with us, it often brings intensity and the realities of the spiritual warfare that is taking place on earth. We experience the wonders of fellowship with Almighty God. But we also draw the attention of the enemy of our souls who resists us and God's work. This often brings tension, intensity, and sometimes conflict.

The disciples and the Apostle Paul witnessed the manifested glory of God. They interacted with heaven and saw glimpses of it. But they were soldiers in the kingdom of God. Their lives were laid down to serve the Lord, His kingdom, and His purpose. The visions were wonderful, but God's visitation into their lives did not make life easier but enabled and strengthened them to fight the good fight. Timothy was told to war a good warfare by the prophecies (1 Tim. 1:18) that were given to him by the elders. Peter tells us to arm ourselves with a mind to suffer (1 Pet. 4:1) for the Lord's sake. When God visits and speaks to you, it does not necessarily follow that you will experience flowery beds of ease. It probably means you should gird up your loins and be prepared to be strong, endure, and persevere.

The Christmas story is a microcosm of the Christian life itself. We see humanity; we see divine intervention and the light of His glory accompanied by great joy and love. But we also see evidence of the darkness that resists God's visitation. That resistance would like to remove Christ from Christmas and make it to be about Santa Clause, jingle bells, and warm, mushy good feelings with a shallow attempt at a fleeting "love your fellow man" feeling but devoid of Jesus Christ, the true meaning of the season and the source of real love.

Stevie Nicks, the lead singer of Fleetwood Mac, has her own version of "Silent Night" on the radio this season. It is a beautiful arrangement. At first, I was impressed but then realized a couple of major and subtle changes. In the original song, one verse ends with, "Christ the Savior is born." A second verse ends with, "Jesus Lord at Thy birth." In the Stevie Nicks version, both of these endings are deleted and replaced with, "It was a silent night; it was a holy night." As I stated earlier, it was not a silent night, but it was holy. Also, it has meaning only in Jesus. The story, the songs, and all the talk about love are empty and shallow without Jesus. The true Christmas story is summed up in these words from scripture:

For God so loved the world that He gave His only begotten
Son, that whoever believes in Him shall not perish but have
everlasting life. (John 3:16)

Herod could not destroy the babe. The devil and the kings of the earth
could not destroy the Lamb slain for our sins. He is now the risen Lord of
Lords and King of Kings who will rule until all His enemies are made a
footstool about His feet. Isaiah's words are true:

> For unto us a Child is born,
> Unto us a Son is given;
> And the government will be upon His shoulder.
> And His name will be called
> Wonderful, Counselor, Mighty God,
> Everlasting Father, Prince of Peace.
> Of the increase of His government and peace
> There will be no end,
> And upon the throne of David and over His kingdom.
> (Isa. 9:6-7)

15

"Behold, You Are There."

IN OUR SPIRITUAL GROWTH, WE NEED TO WALK IN FAITHFUL OBEDI-
ence to the Lord in the full range of experiences, from "pit" to "peak"
and everywhere in between. We grow in spirit and depth as we walk
with Jesus through desert places as well as "green pastures" and as we persevere in faith on stormy seas and in the "deep" as well as the peaceful walk
by "still waters." The psalmist speaks of remembering the Lord from the
Jordan Valley as well as from the heights of Hermon. He experienced the
Lord's lovingkindness in the daytime and His song in the night. Near or
far, high or low, there is no extremity that can separate us from God's love
and care.

Twilla Paris wrote and sang a wonderful song that was popular in
1984. The song tells of the Christian who is amazing and successful in God's
work and in his personal life. The song goes on to say, "They don't know
that I go running home when I fall down. They don't know who picks me
up when no one is around. I drop my sword and cry for just a while. For
deep inside this armor, the warrior is a child."

The song is a good illustration of the two aspects of the struggles and
victories we face in our walk with the Lord. Too often people see the successes and victories which are only the "tip of the iceberg." They don't realize that even the strong sometimes get wounded in the fight. Our battles
are won through faith and obedience. We empower ourselves in the Lord's
presence, and we persevere in the good fight. But the victory is won in the
"prayer closet" in our private time with Jesus. Then later, after the battle
when we are bruised or faint, we return to that secret place of prayer, fellowship, and communion and receive renewed strength, healing, and encouragement.

The Lord told Joshua to "be strong and of good courage." (Joshua 1:6). The Lord repeated the command three times in the same paragraph. "Be strong and of good courage. Do not be afraid, nor be dismayed, for the Lord your God is with you wherever you go." The Lord knew that Joshua would be successful. But He also knew that Joshua, like the rest of us, would face times of being hard-pressed, perplexed, and buffeted by the enemy.

The battles are won in the secret place of God's presence. We wrestle in prayer, intercession, worship, and praise without an audience. There would be no iceberg tip glistening in the sun if it were not for its substance and strength that grew beneath the surface and out of sight.

Of course, we draw strength through fellowship with other believers, from their prayers and all the grace that God gives us through them. But this does not substitute for our own personal walk with Jesus. An overflowing spiritual life includes receiving grace and life from other believers, but we cannot simply live off the overflow of others. We must have our own inner fountain. We draw strength, faith, and encouragement from others ... and from our personal time with the Lord in the secret place of His presence.

> Where can I go from your Spirit? Or where can I flee from
>   your presence?
> If I ascend into heaven, You are there; if I make my bed in
>   hell, behold, you are there.
> If I take the wings of the morning, and dwell in the uttermost
>   parts of the sea, even there Your hand shall lead me and
>   Your right hand shall hold me.
> If I say, "Surely the darkness shall fall on me," even the night
>   shall be light about me;
> Indeed, the darkness shall not hide from You, but the night
>   shines as the day. (Ps. 139:7–12)

Part Two

The Spiritual Battle

16

Courage to Face the Battle

The Cat and the Rat

THIS CHAPTER ILLUSTRATES HOW CHRISTIANS TEND TO ENJOY church but fail to take the message of the gospel out into the world. While Christians have been reluctant to face the world, we need to be aware that the battle may now come to us. The spiritual forces that hate God and His Word will also hate Christians. But to be more specific, they may claim to love God but just hate Jesus Christ and those who follow Him. That's why the Bible calls the end time "man of sin" the "anti-Christ." As the western world tends to unite under some all-inclusive religious unity devoid of Christ, it will begin more and more to attack Christians personally and legally through the laws of the land and thus attempt to silence the testimony of Christians who would share the good news of Jesus Christ and His Word. We are in a spiritual battle. And Christians who have tended to retreat into the four walls of the church need to be aware that the world system will attempt to make those four walls our prison in an effort to keep the message hidden away from the real world and the issues of the day. And sadly, certain laws are being considered that would allow the government to intrude inside those very "four walls" and try to control our very beliefs and practices within the church itself.

Christians have tended to hide within the four walls of the church, but the truth is we cannot avoid the spiritual warfare that affects all of us in the real areas of life we face every day. We will not be able to hide in church. The battle will come to us anyway, and at some point in time, the only way to avoid it will be to deny the Lord either in word or actions or to hide in one of the so-called Christian religious institutions that compromise and deny their very foundation in Christ and the truth of the Bible. My story I am about to share illustrates our need to courageously face the world with the Word of God and the testimony of Jesus Christ. The early Christians prayed for boldness when they were threatened. They also asked for the Lord to grant signs and wonders along with the boldness. That sounds like a great prescription for us today.

The Cat at the Door

When I was just a kid, we had a yard cat that should have been out hunting mice but, instead, was always sitting at the screen door, meowing and whining plaintively, begging for someone to let him in the house. "Meow, meow, meow!" he cried. Translated into English this means, "Let me in. Feed me, pet me, help me, comfort me, and make me happy. I want to go inside where it is comfortable and safe. I don't want to face the world outside."

My dad hated for a cat to sit at the door begging like that. So he pushed the door open and shoved the startled cat out onto the carport. As he walked past, he said, "When I get back, I am going to haul you off to the shopping center." He fully intended to get rid of the cat.

The Fight

About an hour later, I heard a commotion beside the corn barn at the edge of our back yard. I turned my head in time to see about fifteen to twenty squawking chickens flapping their wings, jumping in the air, and scurrying in every direction to flee the water hole that had formerly been a mud-wallow for a few hogs. And among those chickens, I saw that cat in the middle of a backflip somersault a couple feet in the air. I ran over to see what was happening and found the cat locked in mortal combat with a large wharf rat that was as big as the cat. Most of us have seen how a cat will often toy with a mouse, playfully tossing it into the air until he is ready to eat it. In this case, however, the rat had tossed the cat into the air.

I watched this battle until the cat finally killed the rat. He crouched over his prey and maintained a firm grip on the dead rat as he looked up at me with blood flowing from a big cut running across his entire face. His expression almost seemed to say, "I did it! Thank God I'm still alive!" He then proceeded to eat as much of the rat as he could. A couple other cats wandered over and joined the feast. There was rat to go around, and rat left over.

When my dad learned of this event, he decided to keep the cat. There was no trip to the shopping center, and the cat's lifestyle changed dramatically after that. It was as if he had understood my dad's threat to "haul him off." He never again sat whining at the door, and every few days, he would drag up a dead rabbit, or rat, or bird and lay it on the carport, as if to say, "I'm still on the job." The cat, with that ugly trophy scar across his face, stayed with the family a few more years until it died of old age.

The "Door" of the Church

As Christians, we tend to be like that cat. In our focus on self, it is easier for us to "sit at the door" of the church, seeking our own comfort and self-fulfillment rather than facing the tasks and challenges associated with reaching out to people in the real world. We often fear getting involved in the spiritual battle that is involved in the advancement of God's kingdom.

Contemporary culture surrounds us with things that look good, sound good, taste good, and feel good — things that are fun. We want to do what pleases us — DVDs, movies, TV, music, video games, sports, and various amusements. We don't want to face what is difficult, demanding, and tedious. We often expect rewards and fruit when there has been no effort or labor. And we carry this over into our walk with God, expecting Him to bless us, help us, comfort us, etc. without us enlisting to serve Him and His purpose. We want the blessings of the kingdom without the travail and labor involved in the spiritual walk. We avoid anything that causes discontentment, inconvenience, adversity, or pain. We subconsciously think everything in our spiritual walk should be fun, convenient, and focused on "me."

We expect our meetings to entertain us and not be unpleasant. We want positive, shallow messages that do not challenge us. This tends to produce a large crowd of superficial and shallow Christians sitting as spectators, enjoying the performance up front. It seems that the multitudes are not attracted to depth and substance but to glitter, show, and celebrity. They run to the latest thing, the newest thing, and to what gets the most PR. They go after the latest trends and those things that feed their fancy. Church becomes either a buffet or fast food which makes us "fat" rather than the family meal which provides real nourishment, strength, growth, and spiritual substance.

A crowd is a good thing when it is made up of real disciples who want to know and follow Jesus, but a crowd is not necessarily a good thing when the self-centeredness of the people is indulged and when they are not challenged or confronted with truth nor helped to see themselves or the purpose of God. I believe that the Lord does want to bring us in and set us on His lap and embrace us with His love and kindness, but I also think He wants us to quit sitting at the "screen door" and boldly face the challenges and "giants" that await us as we conquer the land with the message of the kingdom of God. Otherwise, as one friend of mine said, "I'll see y'all at the shopping center next week."

I have fought the good fight... (2 Tim. 4:7)

17

"If There's Snakes in There,
There's Fish in There."

If, in the manner of men, I have fought with wild beasts at Ephe-sus...

—1 Corinthians 15:32

For a great and effective door has opened to me, and there are many adversaries.

—1 Corinthians 16:9

Religion versus Harsh Realities

MY DOG WAS CAUGHT COMPLETELY BY SURPRISE IN DEALING with bumble bees and snakes. She was not expecting any real pain or problems other than the fun of the game ... until she was stung by the bee and bitten by the copperhead.

Our Christian walk should be filled with joy and glimpses into the glory of God. But there is also the travail and agony of the battle. Many church people live on a shallow level where church is simply entertaining and fun or complacent ritual and routine. We forget we are in a spiritual battle. When you became a Christian, were you expecting a toaster oven for joining? Were you expecting a tour of duty in Hawaii rather than warfare in the spiritual battlefields of the world? Did you expect the enemy to be fair and play by the rules? Did you expect your Christian friends to be perfect and never disappoint you? Did you expect no surprises, no enigmas, no anomalies? Did you not realize that you might "wake up" one day and say, "Oh God, what happened to me?"

John the Baptist may have felt this way as he sat in a cold, dark prison awaiting his death and questioning his whole life and ministry. He sent word to Jesus asking, "Are you the one or do we look for another?" (Matt. 11:3, paraphrased). Jesus sent encouraging words letting him know that things were progressing according to God's plan. The snake may have bitten your foot, but we are crushing his head. John had done a great work, he had prepared the way, and now Jesus was demonstrating the kingdom of God through miraculous signs and wonders. Jesus, at that time, also reminded the multitudes that the kingdom is not about men in soft garments nor religious people acting like children sitting in the marketplace, playing religious games, and pretending while the real world and reality passes all around them. "The kingdom," He said, "suffers violence, and the violent take it by force" (Matt. 11:12). We get real bruises and real hurts, but we stay in the battle.

Because we have confined our spiritual realities to the inside of the four walls of a church building and placed God behind our religious traditions, choir robes, and candles, it is hard for many to see Him in the harsh realities of everyday life. This is one of the reasons why it is so easy for people to ignore God in real life while checking in with Him on Sunday morning and then inviting Him to the funeral so they can get into heaven if it should happen to exist. Maybe that is one of the reasons the Old Testament had so much blood and sacrifice. People were reminded constantly of life and death and the fact that their spiritual life was intimately tied to the harsh realities of the everyday real world.

"If there's snakes in there, there's fish in there."

When I was a teenager, my friend Mr. Arthur Harrelson and I went fishing in the black waters of Woods Lake just off the Waccamaw River. We paddled with one hand and fished with the other as we slowly maneuvered our small two-man boats through the moss-covered cypress trees and river oaks in the water along the edge of the lake. A tree had fallen over into the water and was lying on its side with half its branches under water and half above water. We slowly guided our boats toward the tree and aimed our hook and line to catch fish that were surely lurking in its branches underwater. The branches and limbs above the water were loaded with snakes, and I kept hearing "ker-plop" and "ker-plop" as I watched many of them drop into the water as our boats approached. Suddenly, I heard splashing and looked around to see that Mr. Harrelson had gotten out of his boat and was wadding waist deep in the black water. He was moving toward the tree and leaning forward with his hook and line dropped into the midst of those limbs.

"Mr. Harrelson!" I said. "What are you doing? There are a lot of snakes in there!"

Never taking his eyes off his cork, he replied, "If there's snakes in there, there's fish in there."

Mr. Harrelson was willing to face the snakes to catch the fish, and he caught more than I did. The same is true in our walk with God. The battle is real, and the enemy is real. Therefore, we should not play games and pretend, but neither should we be afraid and shrink back because of the realities. If the "snakes" are there, the "fish" are there. We should be of good courage and bravely go forward, expecting to be more than conquerors through Christ Jesus. The spiritual battle is real and often difficult and painful, but we will succeed as we continue in faith and patient endurance, placing our trust and confidence in Jesus Christ our Lord.

By your patience possess your souls. (Luke 21:19)

...in all these things we are more than conquerors through Him who loved us. (Rom. 8:37)

Paul and David Law with the lion

18

Standing Together in the Battle

If, in the manner of men, I have fought with beasts at Ephesus...

—1 Corinthians 15:32

Paul Law's Experience with the Lion

THE KENYAN PASTORS SAT ENTHRALLED AS PAUL LAW TOLD THEM of the time he was surprised by the fierce growl of a lion crouching in the bushes in front of him near his missions ranch in the Congo.

He had been told that the creature had left the area, and so he considered it safe to look for the remains of a cow the lion had previously killed and dragged into the bushes. But now the threatening roar announced the presence of the beast.

Paul stopped in his tracks and, without turning his head, was about to quietly give instructions to the three companions following behind him. They, however, were not there. They had already fled to the truck, leaving him alone with the lion. He carefully and slowly walked backwards, keeping his eyes in the direction of a possible attack. He made it safely back to the vehicle to find that the two men who reached the truck first had jumped in, shut the doors, and locked out the third fellow who was now lying in the back of the truck in the fetal position.

The conference pastors sat on the edge of their seat as Paul proceeded to tell how he and his brother David returned later and killed the lion that had become a threat to their children and livestock. Contrasting his faithful brother with the men who had fled in fear, Paul spoke of the strength drawn from friends who stand with us in the battle and in our times of trial. It was a moving and powerful message.

The Rooster and Me

When Paul finished his message, after a short break, it was my turn to speak.

I looked at the group of pastors and said, "Paul Law has told you of the time he was face to face with the lion. I am going to tell you about the time I was attacked." At this point, they leaned forward to hear what harrowing tale I was about to tell. I proceeded, "I am going to tell you about the time I was attacked ... by a rooster!" The audience began to mumble, asking each other, "Did he say 'rooster'?" And then the whole place cracked up as these African pastors all began to laugh. To them a rooster was nothing to fear. A rooster was food, not a predator. It was only a rooster, but it was fierce to me.

I was an eight- or nine-year-old boy at the time, and to me, the event was very traumatic. My Aunt Maggie's old flogging rooster came charging at me, jumping up trying to claw me with those sharp talons. He was not one of those little bantam roosters, but a full-grown, combative, big barnyard boss, almost as big as me. I picked up my cousin's old rusty BB gun and used it as a bat. Every time that rooster jumped up, I would swing that rifle down on his back and knock him back to the ground. I should have swung sideways and hit him upside the head, but I was too afraid to think of that. I struggled for a few minutes until Mrs. Grace Gore, an elderly lady passing by, saw my plight and saved me. It was not much to brag about. I was attacked by a rooster and rescued by an old lady, but the battle was real to me, and she was a beautiful woman on that day.

"For if they fall, one will lift up his companion" (Eccl. 4:10). Both of the above stories illustrate our need to have brothers and sisters to stand with us as we face the issues and trials of life. But even more importantly, they remind us that we should be vigilant in our walk with the Lord so that we are "there" spiritually for those who depend on us and who may need us in their hour of need. There are many today who are facing sicknesses and various mental, spiritual, and physical battles. They need the help, encouragement, and strength that comes from Christian brothers and sisters standing with them in prayer. Many people face their Gethsemanes alone.

Too many Christians lock themselves in the "safety" of the vehicle while others are left outside to fight or die alone. They have not known the love and joy of standing with other Christians and experiencing the power of the Holy Spirit and the love of God manifested when believers stand together in faith and prayer.

> ...the members should have the same care for one another. And if one member suffers, all the members suffer with it. (1 Cor. 12:25–26)

Over this last season, an army of godly believers in many networks have arisen as wonderful examples of prayer warriors standing together in faith to uphold and stand with those who have little strength. It has been heartwarming and encouraging to witness so many networks of prayer demonstrating the love and compassion of Jesus Christ as they have poured out their hearts to God in prayer for those who struggle with sickness, grief, pain, and spiritual battle.

If you are facing the lion or the rooster, whether sickness or other oppressions, you do not have to face it alone. There are many Christians standing ready to pray. Look to Jesus and find those who love Him. There are many faithful believers who will stand with you.

> Praying always with all prayer and supplication in the Spirit, being watchful to this end with all perseverance and supplication for all the saints. (Eph. 6:18)

> For we do not want you to be ignorant, brethren, of our trouble which came to us in Asia: that we were burdened beyond measure, above strength, so that we despaired even of life. Yes, we had the sentence of death in ourselves, that we should not trust in ourselves but in God who raises the dead, who delivered us from so great a death, and does deliver us; in whom we trust that He will still deliver us, you also helping together in prayer for us, that thanks may be given by many persons on our behalf... (2 Cor. 1:8–11)

19

The Ugly Bug on the Wall

The Ugly Bug

ONE EVENING NOT LONG AGO, LAUREL CALLED TO ME, SAYing, "Billy, come here and kill this awful looking bug! What is it?" I rushed to the entrance of the laundry room and saw this ugly black creature on the wall about knee level. It was about the size of a quarter and had two arm-like extensions that resembled miniature crab claws. The larger arm was moving slightly. It made me a little nervous about getting too close to it. It was a bit intimidating.

Laurel said, "Kill it." But I wanted to investigate it further since I had never seen anything like this before. I grabbed a plastic cup and an envelope. I placed the cup over it and slid the envelope between the wall and the cup opening. The creature was then trapped inside.

I went to the front porch and dumped the thing onto the concrete floor in order to get a better view in brighter light. Laurel was still telling me to kill it and not mess with it.

As it lay there, I shined the flashlight on it, and to my surprise, I learned that I had captured a small scrap piece of black plastic trash bag that somehow had been stuck to the wall. We were all somewhat embarrassed to have reacted so dramatically to such a harmless item.

The Meat Is So Raw It Goes "Moo."

I think many of us have heard someone say, "My steak is so rare that it went 'moo' when I cut it."

As I was leaving my mother's house one night, she and my sister Eva gave me a chunk of raw meat that had gone bad and told me to take it home for the dog. I carried it in a bag to my van. The automatic ceiling light was not working in the van, and when I sat the bag of raw meat on the floor between the two front seats, I heard a soft, "Moo, moo," coming from the dark floor where I had set the bag of meat.

It was eerie ... and for a second, I thought there was evil at work. I was about to cast a demon out of the van when I realized I had set the meat on top of a baby's toy that went "moo" when you pressed it.

Once again ... a false alarm.

The Beige Blob Crawling on the Floor

I used to walk in my sleep a lot. Once, I got out of bed in the night and was walking down the hall, very much asleep and in my dream but aware of my environment. I thought there was some kind of ugly, dangerous blob crawling down the hallway. To escape from it, I ran into the bathroom and stood in the tub. I figured if I stayed in the tub and ran some hot water, I'd be safe. So, as I stood there in the tub with the water running, I began to gradually wake up and come to my senses. I said to myself, "There is no such thing as a blob crawling on the floor." Embarrassed and thankful Laurel did not awaken and find me standing in the tub, I sneaked into the bedroom and went back to sleep.

Fear Not

Proverbs 28:1 says that the wicked flee when no one pursues. The Lord's children should be bold as a lion, but Christians sometimes flee when it's not necessary. We fight phantoms that don't really exist. Faith and peace fill our heart and mind when our conscience is clear before God. The Lord is with us. We should not fear.

> ...not in any way terrified by your adversaries, which is to them a proof of perdition, but to you of salvation, and that from God. (Phil. 1:28)

For He Himself has said, "I will never leave you nor forsake you." So that we may boldly say: "The Lord is my helper; I will not fear. (Heb. 13:5–6)

The wicked flee when no one pursues, but the righteous are bold as a lion." (Prov. 28:1)

Behold, I give you the authority to trample on serpents and scorpions, and over all the power of the enemy, and nothing shall by any means hurt you. Nevertheless do not rejoice in this, that the spirits are subject to you, but rather rejoice because your names are written in heaven. (Luke 10:19–20)

I will fear no evil; for You are with me. (Ps. 23:4)

We are subject to fear when our relationship with the Lord is not as it should be. We become vulnerable to the enemy's schemes, lies, and bluffs when we do not know and believe the Scripture. He can scare us and discourage us with a threat or a bluff. "Bluff" means to deter or frighten by pretense or a mere show of strength, to deceive an opponent in cards by a bold bet on an inferior hand with the result that the opponent withdraws a wining hand (*Websters Ninth New Collegiate Dictionary*). This is how the devil operates. He seeks to frighten and intimidate us. This strategy often works on believers who do not know the Scripture, the power of God available to us, and their authority in Jesus' name.

As believers, we need not fear. Christ has delivered us from the kingdom of darkness and transferred us into His kingdom. He defeated Satan at Calvary and stripped him of his power. Satan can only rule over those who choose to serve him and follow him and his ways. To gain advantage and control over Christians, he must use fear, discouragement, deception, accusation, and enticements to sin. He tries to trick us.

We are victorious in Jesus Christ. We don't have to be afraid of the "ugly bug on the wall." We don't have to panic when the "red meat goes moo." And it is also important to know that we don't have to be afraid when a real demon shows up. We have authority, and we can cast it out.

When confronted head-on and in the open, the enemy tries to bluff his way by appearing strong and threatening because he knows he is defeated. He knows that we, as followers of Jesus Christ, are victorious in our God. The problem is that *we* need to know it.

The Lord is my light and my salvation;
Whom shall I fear?
The Lord is the strength of my life;
Of whom shall I be afraid?
When the wicked came against me to eat up my flesh,
My enemies and foes,
They stumbled and fell.
Though an army encamp against me,
My heart shall not fear;
Though war may rise against me,
In this I will be confident. (Ps. 27:1–3)

20

It's Not Safe to Quit

The Surprise Attack

M Y SON, REUBEN, AND I WERE WORKING IN THE YARD ONE SUM-
mer's day a few years ago and stumbled upon a nest of bumble bees
hidden in the ground beside a storage shed out back. Bumble bees
are normally non-aggressive and mind their own business, but they will
attack with vengence if anything disturbs their nest. Reuben and I backed
away, but our dog saw an adventure and fearlessly began to bite and snap
at the buzzing creatures as they flew out of the hole to defend their nest.
This was the dog's first experience with bumble bees, and she was enjoying
it immensely—until she received a couple well-placed stings. She was not
expecting this. The startled dog cried out with a loud yelp and took off running as fast as she could around to the front yard and out of sight. She had
learned her lesson. She found a quiet place, lay on the ground, and began
licking her wounds, assuming the worst was over.

When things calmed down, I returned to investigate the nest. Suddenly, one lone bumble bee came flying out of the hole and right towards
me. I took off running as fast as I could toward the front yard, hoping he
would give up if I ran far enough away from the nest. Nevertheless, when
I looked back, I saw this bumble bee at eye level about three feet behind
me, closing in, and only a couple seconds away from stinging me. Then
suddenly, he inexplicably turned away from me, made a sharp right turn,
and went straight for the poor dog lying quietly in the front yard, minding
her own business. Instantly, I heard the dog give another loud yelp as the
bumble bee stung her again. The dog then jumped up and ran off into the
trees to hide in the bushes. This second attack was an even greater shock

than the first one. Complacent and "minding your own business" will not protect you.

It is not safe to quit.

Just because we get hurt does not mean we should give up and quit or sit on the sidelines and watch. We are in the battle whether we like it or not. The safest place to be is in battle wearing our spiritual armor, not hiding somewhere out of sight "in the front yard."

> Fight the good fight of faith, lay hold on eternal life, to which you were also called... (1 Tim. 6:12)

> Have I not commanded you? Be strong and of good courage; do not be afraid, nor be dismayed, for the Lord your God is with you wherever you go. (Josh. 1:9)

21

Suffering ... or Inconvenience?

Swimming Pool

THROUGHOUT HISTORY, CHRISTIANS HAVE SUFFERED PERSECU-
tion and faced fiery trials for the Word of God, for the testimony of
Jesus, and for righteousness' sake. There are many today who are imprisoned, tortured, persecuted, and put to death for their faith. However,
there are also many of us who have no concept of real suffering for Jesus'
sake. We complain at small inconveniences as if we have paid such a great
price. One pastor's wife said she was suffering for the Lord when she and
her husband left their nice home in California and moved back east into a
house without a swimming pool.

No Toilet Paper

My friend Adam Kuczma was the head of the Methodist Church in Poland
when it was still under communist control back in the days before the Ber-
lin Wall was taken down. He was talking to a lady in America when she
told him, "I want to go to Poland and suffer for Jesus."

"We don't have toilet paper," he responded.

"I don't feel led to go to Poland," was her immediate NO reply.

Taking Up The "Yoke"

On another occasion, Adam told me about the time he was visiting some very poor rural folk in Ukraine and was having a meal in the home of this very humble peasant lady. As she was preparing his meal, he noticed how dirty the table, the glasses, and the dishes were. He saw trash floating around in the milk and told the lady, "My sister, I am sorry, but I cannot drink milk. I will just eat the boiled egg." He assumed that would be safe. But the elderly lady proceeded to peel it for him with dirty hands. After removing the shell, she dropped the egg to the dirty floor, picked it up, and wiped it off on her dirty apron. Realizing the egg was not quite clean enough, she held it to her mouth, licked it "clean" with her tongue, and then handed it to Adam. He thanked her and said, "My sister, I can only eat the yolk. Will you eat the outside white? And I'll just eat the yoke." He was gracious and did not offend this precious lady. He used wisdom in handling a delicate situation.

A Wing and a Prayer

Back in 1969, my friend Larry Rodeffer and I were college students preaching revivals during our summer break from school. It was customary in rural communities for members of the church to invite the guest evangelists for evening meals in their homes. On this one occasion, we sat at the table, enjoying a nice meal. As I lifted my glass and began to drink my iced tea, I noticed an insect wing floating around near the bottom of my glass. I prayed silently, *Lord, how do I handle this?* I did not want to embarrass my hosts, and so I continued to drink the tea without saying anything about the wing. I drank the tea until only about two or three ounces remained in the glass. I then went over to the sink and rinsed it out saying, "I think I'd like to have some ice water."

We learn a lesson here. We should not be complaining over minor inconveniences. We have not yet resisted unto blood. But there are those who are really suffering for Jesus in the world today. Some are imprisoned. Some tortured. There are and will be more martyrs. Others are persecuted economically.

It is difficult for us who live in relative ease to really understand the pain and suffering that many are experiencing. We need to be willing to take up our cross and obey when Jesus asks us to suffer for His name's sake. We also need to daily be in intercession and prayer for the suffering saints around the world. In listing the various pieces of armor needed for our spiritual warfare, the Apostle Paul exhorts us to be *"praying always with all prayer and supplication in the Spirit, being watchful to this end with all perseverance and supplication for all the saints"* (Eph. 6:18).

…one member suffers, all the members suffer with it.
(1 Cor. 12:26)

Remember the prisoners as if chained with them. (Heb. 13:3)

22

The Enraged World

For to you it has been granted on behalf of Christ, not only to be-
lieve in Him, but also to suffer for His sake.

—Philippians 1:29

The "Others"

HEBREWS 11:32–35A GIVES AN IMPRESSIVE LIST OF VICTORIES
and conquests achieved by God's people as they moved in obedience and faith. We emulate their experiences as we read how they
subdued kingdoms, obtained promises, stopped the mouths of lions,
quenched the violence of fire, out of weakness were made strong, became
valiant in battle, and turned to flight the armies of aliens. Some even received their dead raised to life again. As Christians, we stand in faith and
believe that we also will see these same victories accomplished by followers
of Christ today.

However, we must also be prepared to join and stand with the "others" described in the next few verses (Heb. 11:35b-40). These "others" also
stood in faith and were strong in the grace of God, but they did so during
suffering.

> Others were tortured, not accepting deliverance, that they
> might obtain a better resurrection. Still others had trials of
> mockings and scourgings, yes, and of chains and

imprisonment. They were stoned, they were sawn in two, were tempted, were slain with the sword. (Heb. 11:35b–37a)

They are described as obtaining a good testimony through faith while suffering persecution and affliction as they stood faithful to the Word of God and the testimony of Jesus Christ. The Church should be equipped and prepared for both situations: to demonstrate victory and faith in conquests and also to demonstrate faith and victory in their willingness to suffer for righteousness' sake and Jesus' sake and in "loving not their own lives even to death." (Revelation 12:11).

Pastors (especially those on TV) are telling Christians of all the wonderful things they can be and do as they testify of the victories like those in Hebrews 11:32–35. But they should also be preparing Christians to be able to stand in battle, to stand with the "others" of Hebrews 11:35–40 who faced tribulation, persecution, and affliction for the Lord's sake. The Apostle Paul visited the churches, "strengthening the souls of the disciples, exhorting them to continue in the faith, and saying, 'We must through many tribulations enter the kingdom of God.'"(Acts 14:22). We must be prepared to be loved … and hated … sometimes assaulted by those who may be irrationally enraged.

"Wild Beasts"

If, in the manner of men, I have fought with beasts at Ephesus…

—1 Corinthians 15:32

There are wild beasts that cannot be tamed or domesticated. They don't recognize kindness, soft words, or loving speech. If you speak softly to a crocodile or tell him how much you love him, he will still eat you. If you are nice to a rattlesnake, he will still bite you. If you bring honey to a grizzly bear for her cubs, she will kill you. Animals can be brutal and savage. They have no capacity for compassion and will kill with no regret or guilt.

The Apostle Paul said that in the last days people will be brutal and times will be fierce. "Fierce" describes the people as violent and hostile. "Brutal" describes them as cruel, savage, unreasonable, and acting on a physical and emotional level with no compassion or care for others.

The term Paul used to describe the times is the same term the Gospels use to describe the man out of whom Jesus cast a legion of demons. He was fierce and savage, could not be tamed or controlled. He broke chains and cast them asunder and lived wild among the tombs (Matt. 8:29, Mark 5:4). This is descriptive of Satan's goal for man. Man in this state becomes a willing tool in the fight against God and God's people. The Apostle Paul was resisted and assaulted by those whose anger and hostility caused them to behave like wild beasts. They became instruments in the hands of the messenger of Satan sent to buffet. (2 Cor. 12:7).

When the World Is Enraged Against Christians

...I chose you out of the world, therefore the world hates you.

—John 15:19

There are growing forces in our nation that seek to remove God and biblical Christianity from our culture. These forces "preach" against intolerance and hate while exhibiting these very attitudes towards Christians. A culture that calls evil good and good evil will eventually persecute Christians with the same intensity we have witnessed in other nations.

The Bible and Judeo-Christian values in the founding principles of our nation produced a society in which Christians have been relatively comfortable and unthreatened. However, as our culture lays aside biblical values and removes God from its institutions, government, and education, it will begin more and more to despise Christians and hate them because of their commitment to Jesus Christ as the only way to God and because of their stand on moral issues as taught in the Bible. During the Roman persecutions, Christians were called "haters of mankind" because of their disapproval of and refusal to participate in cultural immoralities that were prevalent at the time. There are forces in our culture now moving in that direction. Just as the devil has historically created an irrational and unreasonable hatred toward the Jews, he will also stir up and fuel the same unreasonable and intense hatred toward those who follow Jesus.

We will find ourselves in a social context where those who hate us will not be placated nor appeased. We will not be able to cause them to like us, no matter how much we love them or try to make our message palatable.

The following verses show us how determined and intense can be their hostility toward God, His Word, and His people.

Exceedingly Enraged. Acts 26:9–11

Before he met Christ, Paul was "exceedingly enraged" against Christians and "persecuted" them. "Exceedingly" means "beyond what is required or necessary" and implies extreme and zealous behavior. "Persecute" is from the Greek root word "to chase" and implies an aggressive pursuit. It was not a simple, "I don't like them, and if I happen to stumble upon any of them, I'll punish them." No, it was not casual. It was an aggressive and impassioned hatred accompanied by a legally authorized pursuit in order to imprison and/or kill or force them to recant. The devil seeks to instill this type of attitude and behavior in those who do not know God. We are seeing signs of it in American culture today.

Gnashing with Their Teeth. Acts 7:54, 57

The psalmist said that the wicked gathered, attacked him, and gnashed at him with their teeth. Luke tells us the mob that stoned Stephen cried out with loud voices, stopped their ears, and ran at him, gnashing their teeth. Gnashing is what happens when people are in torment or controlled by anger and hate or in an attack mode. The term is attributed to beasts that snarl and gnash their teeth as they attack their prey. In humans, gnashing of the teeth also implies a frustration that is intermingled with the hate. It is frustrating and foolish to fight God or His people. Jesus said it is like kicking a pitchfork, and I will add "with bare feet."

David said that that his persecutors were like lions, men whose passions were set on fire in their attempts to destroy him.

> My soul is among the lions; I lie among the sons of men who are set on fire, whose teeth are spears and arrows, and their tongue a sharp sword. (Ps. 57:4)

The psalmist prophesied that those who crucified our Lord would be like wild animals in their desire to destroy Jesus.

Many bulls have surrounded Me; Strong bulls of Bashan have encircled Me. They gape at Me with their mouths, like a raging and roaring lion. … For dogs have surrounded Me … But You, O Lord, do not be far from Me … Deliver Me from the sword, my precious life from the power of the dog. Save Me from the lion's mouth and from the horns of the wild oxen! (Ps. 22:12–13, 16, 19–21)

The book of Revelation describes the devil as a dragon enraged and making war against those who have the testimony of Jesus Christ.

And the dragon was enraged … and he went to make war with the rest of her offspring, who … have the testimony of Jesus Christ." (Rev. 12:17)

Why are the nations angry?

The gospel of the kingdom proclaims God's rule as well as His love. The nations are angry at God because they are deceived and because they do not want His rule. Rebellion hates authority. Although God is love, He is also absolute power and authority. In Psalm 2, the nations are angry because they reject His rule and want to be free to do their own will. In Revelation 11:17–18, they are angry because He has taken His great power and imposed His reign, which in this case also means judgment on rebellion and wickedness.

Man going his own way in rebellion will resent the message of the kingdom of God. He will even reject the idea of God's love. So how do we communicate the kingdom of God to a culture in which there are so many who are hostile to it? We must have faith that our communication, when done in wisdom and love, will reach those who are really looking for God. And we must also be prepared for those who will hate us and reject the message, no matter how it is packaged. But still, there are those searching and waiting for the good news. May we boldly and wisely proclaim the risen Lord Jesus to a world that so desperately needs a savior, whether they realize it or not. May we remember the words of Jesus: "A servant is not greater than his master, if they persecuted me, they will also persecute you, if they have kept my word, they will keep yours also." (John 15:20).

Futility of Fighting God

Those who would make futile attempts to fight against God need to take heed to these verses from the Word of God.

> ...In order that the living may know that the Most High
> rules in the kingdom of men, gives it to whomever He will...
> (Dan. 4:17)

> ...the God of heaven will set up a kingdom which shall never
> be destroyed; and the kingdom shall not be left to other peo-
> ple; it shall break in pieces and consume all these [other]
> kingdoms [of man], and it shall stand forever. (Dan. 2:44)

> Why do the nations rage,
> And the peoples plot a vain thing?
> The kings of the earth set themselves,
> And the rulers take counsel together
> Against the Lord and against His Anointed, saying
> "Let us break Their bonds in pieces
> And cast away Their cords from us."
> He who sits in the heavens shall laugh;
> The Lord shall hold them in derision.
> Then He shall speak to them in His wrath.
> And distress them in His deep displeasure. (Ps. 2:1–5)

23

Exorcism in the New Testament Church

Demons Constrained

THE DEMONIC REALM IS REAL. AND ITS OBSCURITY AND LIMITED ability to openly manifest and reveal itself is another evidence of the restraining hand of God. There are spirits everywhere. But why is it they can only show themselves in a limited way? Why not openly show themselves, take charge, and govern directly and in the daylight? Why do they not simply show themselves and make us their open slaves and release a flood of control, fear, pain, and chaos upon us? Why do they tend to skulk around in the dark? Why are they so hidden? The answer is simple. God has confined them to the realm they are in and has given them limited power of influence and operation. Otherwise, they would visibly show up, command obedience, and do as they please as any tyrant and evil dictator would do. But the goodness, wisdom, and mercy of God is evident in His restraining hand. The powers of darkness are hidden because God has ordained it so. However, they do exercise much power and influence over fallen, rebellious, and ignorant mankind. When we reject God's rule, we provide a chair for and give power to the devil. And those who willfully dabble in his deceptive and dark arts such as the occult and the psychic practices will increase the ability of demonic powers to expose themselves. This is evident in paranormal activity, haunted houses, etc.

The Biblical Approach

There are three erroneous approaches to the subject of Satan and demons. The first is the open and active involvement in demonic activity as in the occult, psychic phenomena, the animism of primitive societies, and practices in New Age mysticism. The second erroneous approach is to deny their existence altogether. The third and somewhat irrational approach is that of Christians who believe in the existence of evil spirits because they read about them in the Bible but simply ignore the subject as if the evil spirits described in the biblical examples somehow mysteriously faded into the background and do not relate in any real way to our contemporary society except to entice people to sin. The spiritual realm as described in the Bible is real. If we follow the biblical pattern, we will present the subject of the demonic in a balanced and proper perspective. But still, it is difficult to make it palatable to those who reject the Bible or the reality of the spiritual realm.

I have seen the reality of our authority in Jesus' name and the power He has given us through the Holy Spirit. There is much to be said and taught on the subject. The biblical examples are true, and they are models of what we can do today.

I heard a well-known TV and radio preacher say, "Jesus, the apostles, and the disciples in scripture cast out demons, but we do not do that today." This man loves the Lord and believes the Bible to be true, but he is deceived in this area. The Gospels and the book of Acts give many examples of the early Christians casting out demons. There is no foundation to the proposition that the practice is not necessary today.

The Girl with a Demon

A young girl was involved with a fellow who practiced Satan worship. She had decided to leave home and run away with him. One of her friends, however, brought her to Laurel and me, hoping we could persuade the girl to change her mind. As we sat in our living room, I addressed the girl with these words:

"We are living in a day in which there is much spiritual activity. God is pouring out His Holy Spirit, and we are witnessing a visitation of God's presence and a revival in the gifts of the Holy Spirit and the supernatural presence of Jesus Christ in His Church. But there is also intensification in the realm of darkness which is trying to counterfeit the working of the Holy Spirit. This counterfeit is seen in the surge of demonic activity in the areas of psychic, occult, and New Age activity."

I proceeded to tell the young lady that this rise in spiritual stirrings had created a great hunger in the youth of her generation and that she was faced with a choice. She could turn to the Lord and experience the treasures He is making available, or she could follow her boyfriend in Satan worship and enter the bondage and deception of demonic activity.

At that point in the conversation, an unusual thing began to occur unexpectedly. As I spoke to her, she began to twitch and tremble, and her eyes began to turn up in their sockets. Laurel and I looked at each other, knowing that the Lord's presence had stirred up a demon in the girl. I then told the girl, "What you are experiencing right now is an evil spirit that entered you as a result of your involvement with your boyfriend in Satan worship. We are going to cast it out."

The girl immediately held up both hands with clenched fists and, with a very angry and threatening expression on her face, said, "Don't bother me. There is no telling what I might do!" I was surprised by this unexpected response. As I paused for a second, Laurel immediately spoke to the spirit, saying, "We are not afraid of you. Come out of this girl now!" The threatening and intimidating expression on the girl's face immediately changed from anger to fear and grief. She began to cry as she actually slithered out of the chair and onto the floor. The demon came out of her with groans and cries.

The spirit in the girl first tried to intimidate and frighten us. But it came out of her when faced with the reality of Jesus' presence and our knowledge of the authority we have in His name.

A Superstitious Couple

A few years ago, I was talking with a husband and wife who were beginning to delve into witchcraft and thought they had received communications from dead relatives. I shared the gospel with them, pointing them to Jesus and telling them that the Bible forbids involvement in these occult activities because witchcraft is of the devil and ghosts are not dead people but are, in fact, demons or evil spirits pretending to be dead people.

The enemy was angry that I had shared the truth of the gospel with this couple. Later on that day, I was in my motel room, working at my computer when, all of a sudden, a couple of cans of tuna sitting on the microwave were thrown across the room and onto the floor. It was a spirit trying to frighten me and intimidate me into not sharing the gospel with this couple. I was not afraid but felt the power of the Holy Spirit and the righteous indignation of the Lord rise up within me. I immediately stood to my feet and commanded the spirit to depart, leave, and not come back.

I immediately felt the peace and joy of the Holy Spirit. I took a few minutes to praise the Lord for the truth of His Word, for the efficacy of the blood of Jesus, and for the power and joy of His presence. I then went back to my computer and finished my work.

No Fear

As believers, we need not fear. Christ has delivered us from the kingdom of darkness and transferred us into His kingdom. He defeated Satan at Calvary and stripped him of his power. Our power lies in the power of the Holy Spirit, the cross, the blood of Jesus, the name of Jesus, and the great commission in which Jesus said, "In My name they will cast out demons" (Mark 16:17). The demons tremble; we should not fear.

Satan can rule only over those who choose to serve him and follow him and his ways. To gain advantage and control over Christians, he must use fear, discouragement, deception, accusation, and enticements to sin. Fear and discouragement lead to unbelief and disobedience. Fear paralyses us. Deception leads people astray into error, accusation produces guilt which hinders faith and confidence, and sin causes people to turn away from God.

The enemy also uses our ignorance, which is basically our lack of knowledge. A shallow walk with Jesus and a shallow knowledge of the Bible cause many Christians to be weak, fearful, ineffective, and ill-equipped for spiritual warfare.

But when confronted head-on and in the open by Christians who know their place and authority in Christ, the enemy knows he is defeated. He may try to bluff his way by appearing strong and threatening, but he knows he is defeated. He knows that we, as followers of Jesus, are victorious in our God. The main point I want to emphasize is that we need to know it. "Greater is He that is in [us], than he that is in the world." (1 John 4:4 KJV).

We have powerful weapons.

The authority and power to cast out demons is part of the arsenal of tools Jesus has given to the Church. But sadly, exorcism is one area of ministry that often is either neglected and misunderstood or abused and carried to extremes. Every church leader and minister should be trained in exorcism and should be able to stand with biblical knowledge of the subject, keeping a healthy, balanced perspective. Every follower of Jesus who is filled with the Holy Spirit and instructed in the biblical and wise approach to the subject can experience the presence of God in seeing people delivered from the oppression of evil spirits.

One other important lesson: The examples of exorcisms in movies are perversions of truth. They teach fear and a false reality. They erroneously make it look like the ministers are helpless and the devil has overwhelming power. We do not see that in Scripture. The Bible shows the power of God, Satan's defeat, and our authority over demons. They flee when Holy Spirit-filled Christians speak in the name of Jesus Christ of Nazareth and when the person being ministered to has surrendered to Jesus and actually wants to be free.

> Then the seventy returned with joy, saying, "Lord, even the demons are subject to us in Your name." And He said to them, "I saw Satan fall like lightning from heaven. Behold, I give you authority ... over all the power of the enemy, and nothing shall by any means hurt you. Nevertheless do not rejoice in this, that the spirits are subject to you, but rather rejoice because your names are written in heaven. (Luke 10:17–20)

> Philip went down to the city of Samaria and preached Christ to them. And the multitudes with one accord heeded the things spoken by Philip, hearing and seeing the miracles which he did. For unclean spirits, crying with a loud voice, came out of many ... and many who were paralyzed, and lame were healed. And there was great joy in that city. (Acts 8:5–8)

24

Qualities of the Effective Intercessor

THIS CHAPTER IS FOR THOSE WHO HAVE A BURDEN FOR INTERCESsory prayer and for those who desire a deeper prayer life.

Humility

It takes faith and humility to be an effective intercessor. Most deep intercession takes place in the "prayer closet" and in secret rather than in the spotlight on stage. The intercessor prays unto the Father who sees in secret and who rewards openly (Matt. 6:6). People who are self-centered or selfish or who need to receive recognition and the praises of man will have difficulty with the anonymity of being unheralded in the background. But the intercessor will have the joy of knowing he has access to the heavenly court in the Father's presence.

Spiritual Insight

Intercessors are often given insight into the spiritual realm and are thus armed for effective prayer. From their position as watchmen on the wall, they have a view into the city (insight into the lives of those for whom they pray), and also a view of the surrounding countryside (discernment to see the approaching enemy, his snares, and schemes). Being sensitive to the Holy Spirit, they are able to experience the groaning and intercession Paul speaks of in Romans 8:26 in which intercession is made according to the will and mind of God. This stands in contrast to the shallow, ineffective prayer of those who lack spiritual life and who "beat the air" while missing the target.

Godly Attitude

An intercessor must have a level of maturity that enables him to handle information in a wise and godly manner. He must be able to handle the information and knowledge without being shocked and paralyzed by it. When God gives insight, exposes issues, and entrusts a person with knowledge, that person must be able to maintain sobriety without yielding to pride or being overwhelmed by the information. Shallow, immature, or insincere Christians, when given insight, will tend to engage in gossip rather than prayer. They will criticize and condemn rather than intercede with compassion. A godly attitude is required for effective intercession.

An intercessor must be able to ponder truth without sharing it prematurely with others, without casting pearls before swine, without stumbling, and without sowing discord. Being given insight and knowledge is a great responsibility. Truth must be accompanied by grace (John 1:14), mercy (Ps. 89:14), sobriety (1 Pet. 4:12), and wisdom (2 Tim. 2:15, Prov. 10:20, Isa. 50:4, Prov. 25:11).

Labor and Travail

Intercession involves labor. An intercessor cannot be spiritually lazy. Prayer can be a casual discussion, joyful praise, and peaceful worship, but the Scripture also describes prayer as fighting, wrestling, laboring, and travailing. The battle can sometimes be hard because the intercessor encounters resistance. He stands in the gap for those rushing toward disaster and oblivious to the danger. He may be praying for people who resist God in unbelief, whose walls are broken down with breaches where the enemy can enter unhindered to destroy—were it not for those prayers. The intercessor stands in the way to warn those who are speeding in the dark towards a precipice where the bridge is out. He blocks the road to prevent them from blindly falling headlong to destruction.

The intercessor's work is sometimes hard because he is crying out to God on behalf of those who are too weak to stand up for themselves, too blind (ignorant or oblivious) to realize the danger, or too rebellious to care.

Sometimes he prays for those in sin who have no desire to do the right thing.

There are three types of intercession. The intercessor stands in the gap before the person to prevent him from plunging off the cliff. He stands in the gap before the enemy to prevent the enemy from entering through a breach in the wall. Like Moses, he stands between God and those who would face judgment in order to prevent the wrath and judgment of God (Ezek. 22:30).

Perseverance

The enemy works very hard to hinder, prevent, and discourage Christians from fervent prayer. And our own flesh (human weakness) also gets in the way. That's why Jesus told the disciples that "men ought always to pray and not to lose heart."(Luke 18:1). He knew we would be tempted to give up and quit. We tend to think a task is not of God unless it is easy. We are like the disciples who fell asleep in the Garden of Gethsemane while Jesus was in the agony of intercession. The intercessor must realize that prayer is not always goosebumps, "glory clouds," and thrills but can also be agony, labor, and warfare that require us to press in, knowing that God responds to faith and importunity. Jacob wrestled through the night and told the Angel of the Lord, "I will not let You go unless You bless me" (Gen. 32:26). Lately in my own prayer life in my desperation, I have prayed, "Lord, I will not let you go unless you bless me ... because I cannot go unless you bless me!"

When We Don't Know Why

An intercessor may sometimes be led to pray when he senses something but doesn't know what "it" is. In the garden of Gethsemane, Jesus told the disciples to watch and pray. They had no idea what was coming, even though He had told them. They must have seen His agony and struggle of the moment. But still they were not moved to action. They were troubled but did not understand why. They suffered with two problems that often prevent us from effective prayer: First of all, they did not feel like praying. And secondly, they did not realize the hour that was upon them. We start to pray, but suddenly, we are sleepy or dull of mind. We are troubled, but still, we are comfortable enough to fall asleep. Like Lot, we may walk in righteousness but in our spiritual insensitivity are oblivious to the fire that is coming. If we could see into the spiritual realm and really know the activity occurring there, we would wake up, fall on our face, and cry out to God. Thank God for the "Abrahams" who enter the council room and hear the Lord's voice telling them the seriousness of the hour and the intensity of what lies ahead. Without Abraham's prayers, Lot might have perished in the fire along with the people of Sodom and Gomorrah (Gen. 19:29).

The intercessor is often given prophetic insight to see into the spiritual realm and is able to pray with knowledge and understanding. But he must also be prepared for those times when Jesus tells him to "watch and pray" but does not tell him why. Those are times when the intercessor prays in the Holy Spirit and waits before the Lord.

25

Some Keys to Successful Spiritual Warfare

1 Timothy 1:18–20, Ephesians 6:10–18

BELOW IS A LIST OF PRINCIPLES THAT WILL BE HELPFUL IN YOUR walk with the Lord and in facing the adversities and difficulties of life.

Realize we are on a battleship and not a cruise ship.

We must face Og (the enemy at the border), cross the Jordan, and deal with giants in the land we will possess. Christians often tend to expect victory without battle … and if there is adversity, they tend to expect battle without victory. If we continue and stand in faith, we will see battle … but also victory (1 Cor. 15:32, 16:9).

Don't be disillusioned by adversity, hardship, and struggles of battle.

We are called to patiently endure and persevere. In the beginning, we are raring to go but with naïve and untested faith. We are often naïve to the potential carnalities and failures in ourselves and others.

Those who don't face these issues redemptively risk becoming "burnt stones," (Nehemiah 4:2) afraid to try again. The first time we eagerly went Lamaze or all natural. But after a few rounds of perplexity and disillusionment, we stand back and say, "I want an epidural."

We must get up and keep going (Acts 14:19–20; 2 Cor. 4:8-9).

Realize that in your walk with God, you have to deal with people (Psalm 18:1–3, 43, 47-48).

The human factor complicates matters and requires more faith on our part. We deal with spirits from a position of spiritual authority, but we face men from a different perspective. We have no authority or control over another person's will. We can cast out demons; we cannot cast out people. It takes faith and godliness to deal with people.

Therefore, demons hide behind and work through people. Dealing with people puts us in the position of having to call on God, stand in faith, walk in the Spirit, and persevere, trusting God to give us wisdom and grace and help.

When David played his harp, the evil spirit fled—but Saul did not. In dealing with Saul, David had to call upon and trust God, flee to the strongholds, and persevere as he waited for God to judge Saul.

Dealing with people puts us in the position of having to fight according to the rules while the enemy and his crowd cheat and hit below the belt, which makes the person of integrity feel at a disadvantage (Isa. 59:15). It forces us to fight *spiritually*. It places extra demand for faith on our part since we are not to get in the flesh using carnal weapons. This takes the battle out of our hands and places it in God's hands (2 Cor. 10:1–6).

Be prepared for intensities, complexities, perplexities, anomalies, and surprises.

It is not unusual for us to go through times of distress or perplexity in which we experience things we did not expect when the pangs of distress press upon us.

Sometimes we say to the Lord, "Where did you go?" (Psalm 13).

In our discouragement and dark moments, we are disappointed and lose hope and think the Lord is not aware of what's happening. The two disciples felt their hope was lost (Luke 24:21).

Sometimes we feel like "the wretched man" (Rom. 7:24, 25; Luke 22:31–32, 60–62).

Isaiah said, "I have labored in vain, I have spent my strength for nothing…" (Isa. 49:4).

"But Zion said, 'The Lord has forsaken me, and my Lord has forgotten me'" (Isa. 49:14).

Like John in prison, we say, "Are you the Coming One, or do we look for another?" (Matt. 11:3).

John the Baptist had experienced the prophetic word (Luke 1:76–80). He had seen the glory of Jesus' baptism (John 1:29–39). He gladly gave his followers to Jesus and was willing to lay down his preeminence because he knew Jesus was the Christ (John 3:22–30). Yet in his dark moment of prison doubt and facing death, he sent to Jesus, asking, "Are you the Coming One, or do we look for another?" (Matt. 11:3).

The Lord is merciful. He knows our frame and understands that we are but dust (Ps. 103:14). To all these questions, He proclaims His love and faithfulness and brings us through if we persevere in faith. He will come and will not be silent.

We must be faithful in all conditions from the distress of the pit to the glories of the peak and everywhere in between. David wrote Psalms from the mountain and from the valley. The anointing was upon him even when it felt like the Lord had forgotten and forsaken him. Jesus may be for a moment out of your sight, but you are never out of His sight.

Sometimes we face contrasting extremes simultaneously. We experience trials that make us feel God has left us while at the same time seeing great demonstrations of His presence and miraculous help. Circumstances change, but our God does not change. His love is truly steadfast and endures forever. Jesus said, "Lo, I am with you always, even to the end of the age" (Matt. 28:20).

Have a heart for God's purpose rather than a self-centered focus.

A self-centered focus will "sideline" you from the real battle. Self-centeredness distorts perception. It causes you to be focused on yourself without actually seeing yourself. It will be a distraction from your ability to see reality, the heart of God, and the real needs and situations around you. Because we can be so blind to ourselves, we must be truly surrendered for God to be able to show us ourselves. He wants to reveal the way of the cross to us and free us from the way of self.

Trust in the Sovereign God who is able to procure and secure, to uphold and defend.

We must always remember that God is able to do exceedingly, abundantly above all we could ask or think. Nothing is too hard for the Lord. *He* is God Almighty. His greatness is unsearchable and beyond our ability to comprehend.

King Saul lost sight of this reality and clung to his position as king while God was asking him to lay it down. God had rejected Saul and had chosen David. Saul, in his futile attempt to hold the throne, increased his rebellion by trying to kill David. Those who serve the Lord must be willing to lay even their ministry and service upon the altar at the feet of Jesus. We obediently take up what He gives us, and we humbly lay down what He asks us to relinquish. Obedience must come before ministry and position.

Wait upon God to judge.

We generally want to pass judgment and execute vengeance (but we cloak it with the desire for justice) upon our oppressors. When people suffer at the hands of the wicked, they often forget that God is the Righteous Judge. Everyone will ultimately answer to Him.

When Jesus was on trial and being crucified, He committed Himself to Him who judges righteously. Your oppressors will ultimately answer to God if they do not repent. Meanwhile, we must leave room for the wrath of God and trust Him to administer it wisely and in His time. The Lord says, "When I choose, I judge."

Engage the Lord.

Press into the Lord in faith, prayer, and intercession. Maintain real and intimate fellowship with the Lord in all that you face in life. This includes Bible reading and prayer as part of our daily walk with Him. We should make special effort to enter our prayer closets and sit at the feet of Jesus when we face adversities and various trials.

Engage the Lord *first*.

Wrestle with God, as Jacob did, before you wrestle with the devil or other people. The main characters on the stage of your life are you and God. The devil and other people are secondary. We must make sure the slate is clean in our relationship with the Lord and make sure we hear what He is saying to us before we "attack" others or the devil. Remember, we move heaven in order to move earth. Those who fail to seek the Lord and call on Him in their struggles with others or with difficult situations will find themselves frustrated, spiritually drained, disillusioned, and discouraged. Therefore, deal with God before dealing with others.

Sanctify the Lord.

This means that in our daily life, we set the Lord apart from and above all else so that our spiritual eyes are always on Him. No matter what people say or do, no matter what circumstances fall before us, we see the Lord. We respond to everything knowing He is watching and listening. So that in all things, we try to please Him rather than reacting to people and circumstances. We tend to be more obedient when we realize He is watching us.

Realize that you are in God's hands ... not in the hands of people or the devil.

Paul did not see himself as prisoner of the Romans, but rather a "prisoner of the Lord." Joseph was thrown into a pit, sold as a slave, and put in prison on his trip to Egypt. But his testimony was that "God sent him." Because he trusted in God and saw the Lord in control of his life, God caused all things to work to Joseph's good and God's purpose. He became ruler of Egypt next to Pharaoh. We are in God's hands, even when lawless hands are grabbing at us.

Avoid the victim mentality.

A victim's mentality places your life into the hands of other people. If others are responsible for your condition, then you will depend on them to get you out of it, but they will not. You will blame them, wait for them, and sit helpless, bitter, and angry. Accept responsibility for yourself. Acknowledge your own sin, bad decisions, and wrong responses. Then seek the Lord and discover the way out. Don't blame others. Look to the Lord in faith and rise to your destiny. You may have been oppressed and treated badly. Joseph experienced that. But he still fulfilled God's plan for his life. You can too. But you will not succeed if you are hamstrung with a victim's mentality.

Walk in God's ways to accomplish God's will.

It is not enough just to know what God wants in a situation; we must also know how He wants us to accomplish it. The devil tries to keep us from knowing God's will. But when we discover it, the devil then offers suggestions on how to do it. We must walk in the Spirit and godliness. Often Christians think that because they are right in a particular matter, they can throw a fit and get in the flesh to get done what they think the Lord wants done. If the Lord told you that He wanted you to prosper, you would not then go out and rob a bank. You would then work and be diligent in life — you would not turn to crime. We must apply the same principle to how we behave in life, in church, and in other matters.

Be sober.

Sobriety means sound judgment rooted in the right spirit. When we maintain a godly attitude, we are able to hear the voice of the Holy Spirit and have good discernment. A wrong spirit, such as hatred, bitterness, resentment, and anger, will cloud our understanding and perception. Spiritual laziness and complacency will also fog our ability to discern and see clearly.

Maintain a humble and contrite spirit.

The Lord will not despise a broken and contrite heart. Arrogance and pride will cause God to resist you. Pride will bring contention. It will also make you susceptible to the suggestions of the devil. A humble and contrite spirit will be quick to repent of sin and will be teachable and open to correction and instruction.

Be strong and courageous.

Fear not. Know that the Lord will not leave you nor forsake you. Those heroes of faith were not always naturally strong, but rather "out of weakness were made strong" (Heb. 11:34) and that by faith. Paul tells us to be strong in the grace of God. David "strengthened himself in the Lord." We go from strength to strength as we hunger for the Lord and seek Him. Faith, prayer, fellowship, and the Bible are tools through which we tap into the strength God gives. We strengthen ourselves as David did. God strengthens us, and we strengthen one another.

Don't be angry at God.

Do not tempt the Lord by accusing Him of evil, injustice, and unfaithfulness. Ascribe greatness to the Lord. Praise Him for His great and abundant mercy and manifold grace. Praise the Lord for He is good and His steadfast love endures forever.

We often fail to recognize God's power and greatness. But also, we fail to see His kindness, goodness, love, and wisdom. In Israel's journey across the wilderness on their way to Canaan, they rebelled and sinned against God many times. But amazingly, the manna never ceased. It was there every day. Nehemiah 9:18–21 says that even when the Israelites made a molded idol and worked great provocations, God did not forsake them. The pillar of cloud did not depart from them by day to lead them on the road, and the pillar of fire was there every night to show them light. The Lord did not withhold His manna from their mouth, and He gave them water for their thirst. The manna never ceased.

This dynamic happens in our lives also. We tend to be blind to the mercies and longsuffering of the Lord shown to us each day. We should be thankful to Him for all His benefits and not be quick to charge Him foolishly. The writer of Proverbs says, "The foolishness of a man twists his way, and his heart frets against [blames] God" (19:3). We should trust Him and ascribe goodness, greatness, love, and longsuffering to our God.

Have an honest heart.

Spiritual fruit is borne from an honest heart (Luke 8:15), one that loves truth and faces reality. The Lord desires truth in the inward parts (Ps. 51:6). We must be honest with ourselves so that we do not deceive ourselves. Loving the truth (reality as God sees it) helps with our discernment and understanding. Loving unrighteousness leads to deception (2 Thess. 2:9–12).

26

Our Disposition During Persecution

THE NEW TESTAMENT CHRISTIANS WERE AS AMAZING IN THEIR SUF-
fering as they were in their power.

Every Christian who stands on the Word of God and testimony of Jesus Christ should read the Bible verses listed below. These verses describe how Christians should handle persecution, and they encourage us to stand courageously in faith and love when we are reviled, falsely accused, and persecuted. We listen to the words of Jesus and follow the examples of those first believers who experienced extraordinary grace enabling them to display exemplary behavior in the face of great persecution. We see in them no signs of hate, bitterness, or even discouragement. They were as amazing in their suffering as they were in their power.

And in more recent history, we have been encouraged by a great cloud of witnesses including people like Richard Wurmbrand who suffered at the hands of both the Nazis and the communists and Corie Ten Boom who, along with her family, suffered under the Nazi invasion of Holland. They demonstrated great love and endurance. Our desire and prayer is that we will find grace to follow the godly examples of those biblical heroes as well as those of recent history.

Rejoice and be glad; count it as an honor.

> These things I have spoken to you, that in Me you may have peace. In the world you will have tribulation; but be of good cheer, I have overcome the world. (John 16:33)

Blessed are those who are persecuted for righteousness' sake, for theirs is the kingdom of heaven. Blessed are you when they revile and persecute you, and say all kinds of evil against you falsely for My sake. Rejoice and be exceedingly glad, for great is your reward in heaven, for so they persecuted the prophets who were before you. (Matt. 5:10–12)

Beloved, do not think it strange concerning the fiery trial which is to try you, as though some strange thing happened to you; but rejoice to the extent that you partake of Christ's sufferings, that when His glory is revealed, you may also be glad with exceeding joy. If you are reproached for the name of Christ, blessed are you, for the Spirit of glory and of God rests upon you. On their part He is blasphemed, but on your part He is glorified. (1 Pet. 4:12–14)

…and when they had…beaten them, they commanded that they should not speak in the name of Jesus, and let them go. So they departed from the presence of the council, rejoicing that they were counted worthy to suffer shame for His name. (Acts 5:40–42)

Forgive

…and they cast him out of the city and stoned him… And they stoned Stephen as he was calling on God and saying, "Lord Jesus, receive my spirit." Then he knelt down and cried out with a loud voice, "Lord, do not charge them with this sin." And when he had said this, he fell asleep. (Acts 7:58–60)

For to this you were called, because Christ also suffered for us, leaving us an example, that you should follow His steps: Who committed no sin, nor was deceit found in His mouth, who when He was reviled, did not revile in return; when He suffered, He did not threaten, but committed Himself to Him who judges righteously. (1 Pet. 2:21–23)

Persevere and Endure

> And daily in the temple, and in every house, they did not cease teaching and preaching Jesus as the Christ. (Acts 5:42)

> ...they stoned Paul and dragged him out of the city, supposing him to be dead. However, when the disciples gathered around him, he rose up and went into the city. And the next day he departed with Barnabas to Derbe. And ... preached the gospel to that city and made many disciples... (Acts 14:19–21)

Worship and Praise

> ...the magistrates tore off their clothes and commanded them to be beaten with rods. And when they had laid many stripes on them, they threw them into prison, commanding the jailer to keep them securely. Having received such a charge, he put them into the inner prison and fastened their feet in the stocks. But at midnight Paul and Silas were praying and singing hymns to God, and the prisoners were listening to them. (Acts 16:22–25)

Appointed to suffering: Realize it is somehow necessary (in the mystery and wisdom of God).

> For to you it has been granted on behalf of Christ, not only to believe in Him, but also to suffer for His sake... (Phil. 1:29)

> For to this you were called, because Christ also suffered for us, leaving us an example... (1 Pet. 2:21)

> When He opened the fifth seal, I saw under the altar the souls of those who had been slain for the word of God and for the testimony which they held. And they cried with a loud voice, saying, "How long, O Lord, holy and true, until You judge and avenge our blood on those who dwell on the earth?" Then a white rob was given to each of them; and it was said to them

that they should rest a little while longer, until both the number of their fellow-servants and their brethren, who would be killed as they were, was completed." (Rev. 6:9–12)

...he is a chosen vessel of Mine to bear My name before Gentiles, kings, and the children of Israel. For I will show him how many things he must suffer for My name's sake.
(Acts 9:15–16)

Commit yourself to God the Righteous Judge.

...who, when He was reviled, did not revile in return; when He suffered, He did not threaten, but committed Himself to Him who judges righteously. (1 Pet. 2:23–23)

Therefore let those who suffer according to the will of God commit their souls to Him in doing good, as to a faithful Creator. (1 Pet. 4:19)

For this reason I also suffer these things; nevertheless I am not ashamed, for I know whom I have believed and am persuaded that He is able to keep what I have committed to Him until that Day. (2 Tim. 1:12)

Stand in faith to pass the test. (Sometimes it is a test.)

Do not fear any of those things which you are about to suffer. Indeed, the devil is about to throw some of you into prison, that you may be tested, and you will have tribulation ten days. Be faithful until death, and I will give you the crown of life. (Rev. 2:10)

Simon, Simon! Indeed, Satan has asked for you, that he may sift you as wheat. But I have prayed for you that your faith should not fail. (Luke 22:31)

Be courageous; do not fear.

Do not fear any of those things which you are about to suffer. Indeed, the devil is about to throw some of you into prison, that you may be tested, and you will have tribulation ten days. Be faithful until death, and I will give you the crown of life. (Rev. 2:10)

...and not in any way terrified by your adversaries, which is to them a proof of perdition, but to you of salvation, and that from God. (Phil. 1:28)

For God has not given us a spirit of fear, but of power and of love and of a sound mind. Therefore do not be ashamed of the testimony of our Lord, nor of me His prisoner, but share with me in the sufferings for the gospel according to the power of God... (2 Tim. 1:7–8)

Do not be ashamed.

Therefore do not be ashamed of the testimony of our Lord, nor of me His prisoner, but share with me in the sufferings for the gospel according to the power of God. (2 Tim. 1:8)

For I think God has displayed us, the apostles, last, as men condemned to death; for we have been made a spectacle to the world, both to angels and to men. We are fools for Christ's sake... We are weak ... we are dishonored! To the present hour we both hunger and thirst, and we are poorly clothed, and beaten, and homeless. And we labor, working with our own hands. Being reviled, we bless; being persecuted, we endure; being defamed, we entreat. We have been made as the filth of the world, the offscouring of all things until now. I do not write these things to shame you, but as my beloved children I warn you. ... Therefore I urge you, imitate me. (1 Cor. 4:9–16)

Commend yourselves as servants of God.

"But in all things we commend ourselves as ministers of God" (2 Cor. 6:4–10). As "servants of God," we do not represent ourselves but are his ambassadors. Persecution is aimed at the word of God and the testimony of Jesus. We do not react in a self-centered way and make ourselves the focus.

The three Hebrew men were protected in the fire because they saw themselves as "servants of the Most High" (Dan. 3:17). Your behavior and reaction to life are determined or affected by whom you serve. If you are serving self and self-interest, you will react in the flesh. If you are serving the Lord, you will conduct yourself with grace, faith, and godliness. You will "commend yourselves as servants of God."

Maintain personal integrity (so the enemy cannot justifiably assault you for corruption).

> So the governors and satraps sought to find some charge against Daniel concerning the kingdom; but they could find no charge or fault, because he was faithful; nor was there any error or fault found in him. Then these men said, "We shall not find any charge against this Daniel unless we find it against him concerning the law of his God." (Dan. 6:4–6)

> But let none of you suffer as a murderer, a thief, an evildoer, or as a busybody in other people's matters. (1 Pet. 4:15)

Love not your life unto death.

> And they overcame him by the blood of the Lamb and by the word of their testimony, and they did not love their lives to the death. (Rev. 12:11)

> And see, now I go bound in the spirit to Jerusalem, not knowing the things that will happen to me there, except that the Holy Spirit testifies in every city, saying that chains and tribulations await me. But none of these things move me; nor do I count my life dear to myself, so that I may finish my race

with joy, and the ministry which I received from the Lord Jesus, to testify to the gospel of the grace of God. (Acts 20:22–24)

Persecution is sometimes related to judgment, beginning at the house of God.

For the time has come for judgment to begin at the house of God. ... Therefore let those who suffer according to the will of God commit their souls to Him in doing good, as to a faithful Creator. (1 Pet. 4:17, 19)

Remember and pray for those who are suffering persecution for Christ's sake.

Remember the prisoners as if chained with them—those who are mistreated—since you yourselves are in the body also. (Heb. 13:3)

But now God has set the members, each one of them, in the body just as He pleased. ... And if one member suffers, all the members suffer with it; or if one member is honored, all the members rejoice with it. (1 Cor. 12:18, 26)

Conclusion

Most of us feel weak and unable to live up to the standard presented in the verses quoted above. I must, therefore, remind the reader that God will give grace as it is needed for those who call upon Him in faith and who sincerely follow Him with their whole heart. The writer of Hebrews tells us that "out of weakness [they] were made strong" (Heb. 11:34). Some, by the grace of God, were enabled to work wonders and do great exploits. Others were given grace and strength for suffering. Our Lord will give us what we need as the occasions arise.

Part Three

Some Stories and Testimonies

27

Healed of Obsessive-Compulsive Disorder

THE FOLLOWING PARAGRAPHS TELL MY PERSONAL TESTIMONY OF how Jesus revealed Himself to me and healed me of mental torments I went through, suffering silently during my youth. I pray this will speak to and encourage others who may be experiencing similar afflictions.

No one knew the mental torment I was going through, and I managed to keep it hidden from my parents, sisters, and friends through all my years in elementary, junior high, and high school. The problem was a blend of some sort of panic disorder accompanied by an obsessive-compulsive disorder.

I first experienced it in the car returning home from my tonsillectomy surgery. As the car approached our home at the crossroads in Longs, South Carolina, I suddenly felt different and strange in the head. I thought to myself, *Something isn't right.* I was only eleven or twelve years old and did not have the maturity or vocabulary to explain to anyone that my mind was different. I suffered with the problem for another six years and told no one about it until I told my wife, Laurel, when I was twenty-two years old.

After that first experience, the next major episode was a full-force attack while I was sitting in my sixth-grade classroom. I suddenly felt crazy. This weird, unexplainable consciousness came over me, accompanied by a physical reaction in which everything turned green for a couple seconds. Everything literally felt surreal. I immediately went to the teacher and said, "Something is wrong. I don't feel right." She called my dad who picked me up from school and took me to our family doctor.

"What's wrong today?" the doctor asked.

Unable to explain it, all I could say was, "I felt green." It is difficult for an adult and impossible for a child to describe to anyone what it feels like when the mind or consciousness goes into that surreal state. One person described it as "feeling separated." But I could not communicate this to the doctor.

Turning to my father, he said, "You know how kids are. They look for ways to get out of school." So I went home suffering with a real malady that would silently torment me regularly and intermittently for the next six years, and no one knew about it but me.

Most of the time, I felt normal, but these weird mental torments would occur intermittently and occasionally every day or so. I remember thinking, *I am going crazy. Everyone has such high hopes for me, but I am going to end up in a mental institution. Daddy and Mama and everyone will be so disappointed.* It was frightening, and I did not know how to tell anyone about it. I did not know there was a name for the condition and that there were others who suffered with it. I was just a little kid who thought he was going crazy.

Compulsive Disorder

Then came the obsessive-compulsive behavior. It manifested itself in many ways, all of which were tormenting and inconvenient. I went through a phase in which I would compulsively hum some song or familiar tune at the table during the family meal. My father would look at me with a stern look and say, "Billy, stop humming." I would immediately stop, but since the humming was compulsive and done almost unconsciously, a minute or two would pass, and I would look over and see my dad staring at me again, this time more frustrated. "Billy, I said to stop the humming." My mother and father saw the problem only as a bad habit. They had no idea the problem was deeper.

There were many other symptoms. If I ran around a tree or the old well in the front yard while playing with other children, I would be compelled to retrace my steps back around the tree or the well. It was as if there was an imaginary line attached to my back and anchored to some other point of reference in the yard. I had to retrace my path so I would not tangle this imaginary rope or wrap it around the tree or the well. I could not walk past a door without stopping to look behind it. There were times I had to swing a door back and forth, looking behind it ten or fifteen times before I could leave it. Everything had to be symmetrical. I could not let my shoes fall to the floor and leave them as they lay. They had to be side by side, completely straight and parallel. I could not leave a piece of clothing or sock in the opening of a partially closed drawer. When writing, I had to retrace any word or letter where the ink had skipped or was not as dark as the rest of the line, sometimes tracing a word or sentence many times. I don't know how I managed to keep all of these problems hidden from family and friends for so many years.

Obsessive Disorder

The obsessive side of the problem attacked me most severely when I was in the tenth grade. That was the year I tried so hard to walk with the Lord and apply myself spiritually. I took my Bible to school. I studied it and shared my faith with others. But I found myself beginning to be tormented with obsessive tendencies. My thoughts began to race uncontrollably and run on their own, especially in the area of my Christian experience. I felt myself losing control, and it scared me. As a result, I decided to not be spiritually aggressive. I was afraid of going insane.

My eleventh-grade year of high school, therefore, was my period of lukewarm Christianity, a time when I backed away from real spiritual activity. I was simply a nominal church member. I believed in Jesus, tried to behave, but was reserved about my walk with God. I survived the year but decided I could not live a life without an intimate, real, and deep walk with the Lord. I did not want to live a life without God, but I was afraid that if I tried to be spiritually aggressive, I would become obsessive again and go crazy. I had to have a supernatural answer. I decided to go directly to God.

On the Housetop

It was the summer before my senior year in high school. I was seventeen years old. I came home one Saturday night and decided it was time to reach out to God for help. In desperation to get into His presence, I went outside and climbed on top of a storage house in our back yard. I lay on the roof, looked up toward the stars, and called out to God.

"Lord Jesus, You are God. I know You are there and You hear me. You know me better than I know myself. You know the struggle that I have been dealing with. I cannot live without You. But I don't want to risk going crazy like when I tried to serve you before. Therefore, Lord, I need you to visit me, touch me, and give me an experience with You that will make me what I am supposed to be. And show me what You want me to do for You with my life." I knew He was hearing the cry of my heart.

Jesus Reveals Himself

The next day, I went into the woods and prayed. I remained isolated most of the day just reaching out to the Lord.

Later that evening, I was riding with my Uncle W.D. in his pickup truck. I turned to him and said, "W.D., I think the Lord is calling me to preach." Then suddenly and powerfully, God answered my prayers. Jesus revealed Himself in that pickup truck. He was there. The Holy Spirit moved in me, and I was instantly changed, and Jesus became so real, as if I could reach out and physically touch Him. In that moment, He said, "That's right. I am calling you to preach, and I am with you." I began to bounce up and down on the truck seat and rejoice. The revelation of Jesus Christ in that moment transformed me.

W.D. stopped at the Dairy Maid, a hang-out for high school kids in the small town of Loris, South Carolina back in the 60s. I jumped out of the truck and in my excitement ran up to some of my high school friends and began telling them, "I just had an experience with Jesus! He is real! He is alive! And He has touched me! And He has also called me to preach the gospel!"

Jesus Healed Me

I knew from that moment that the Lord's call was on my life. In the days that followed, I began to realize that He had also healed me. The panic disorder and the compulsive-obsessive torments were gone. I was a new person. Jesus had become so real it seemed I could reach out and touch Him, and I was free from the mental vexations that had afflicted me for so many years. That was the beginning of a wonderful adventure in faith and walking with God.

I shared with many the testimony of my intimate encounter with Jesus, how He visited and touched me and called me into His service. But I did not say anything yet about the healing I had experienced. The first person with whom I shared that was my wife, Laurel, when I was twenty-two years old, about four or five years after my healing.

There are some people who can ignore God and somehow live their lives with what appears to be relative ease. There are some Christians who appear to be satisfied and comfortable as lukewarm Christians. But there are also those for whom there is no "safe" area outside of God. Their choice is to walk with God or face disaster. I was among that group. To survive and live a normal life, I must maintain my walk with the Lord. I recognize and appreciate the grace of God which has enabled every success and strength in my life. I also see so clearly the precipices, snares, pits, and help-less emptiness that would have been my portion had I not met Jesus Christ. He is truly my Lord and, in its most real sense, my *Savior*.

28

God's Provision for an Unusual Trip

"Let me not be ashamed."

D URING THE LATTER PART OF 1972, LAUREL AND I AND OUR FIRST child were living in South Carolina. We were preparing to drive to California to attend her sister's wedding but had only enough money for one way. We sought the Lord and felt very strongly that He wanted us to make the trip. However, I did not want to be irresponsible and embarrass myself by being stranded in California and having to call on family or friends for finances to return home. So we prayed and began our journey with peace and faith, knowing we had heard from God. The Lord would provide for the trip back, and we were excited to see how He would do it. We agreed that we would not tell anyone of our need but would simply pray and trust the Lord. This would give greater proof that God was leading us.

As we drove toward the West Coast, I prayed two verses of scripture every day and throughout the day. Those two prayers were directly from Psalm 25.

O my God, I trust in You; Let me not be ashamed. (Ps. 25:2)

Let me not be ashamed, for I put my trust in You. (Ps. 25:20)

The Lord's Promise

We arrived in California, attended the wedding, visited Laurel's family, and spent time with friends from the church there. Soon it was time to return home. We had no money, and I was getting nervous. We told no one about our situation, and no one knew our pockets were empty. So, one night after everyone went to sleep at Laurel's parents' home, I went downstairs and began to pray. "O my God, I trust in You; let me not be ashamed. Let me not be ashamed, for I put my trust in You." I also told the Lord that I had to leave the next day. After spending some time praying, I opened my Bible to Isaiah 53 and read to the end of the chapter. Then suddenly, I felt a very strong sense of the Holy Spirit's presence. And in my heart, I heard Him say, "I am about to speak to you." So, I very carefully looked at my Bible and began to read Isaiah 54. The words in verse 4 leaped out at me like an audible voice:

> Do not fear, for you will not be ashamed; Neither be disgraced, for you will not be put to shame.

I began to rejoice, praise, and thank the Lord. He was assuring me that Laurel's and my prayers were being answered. He was going to provide, and I would not be put to shame.

The return trip begins.

The next day, Laurel's sister, Mary, gave us fifty dollars as a "thank you" for a gift we had given her the year before. We were grateful to the Lord for this provision and drove across the California desert feeling like Israel on their journey across Sinai. The Lord was going to provide on this trip the same way He provided for Israel with the manna—one step at a time, as it was needed.

Our first stop was in Phoenix, Arizona. We spent the night with friends who were on the board of regents at Oral Roberts University. I told Laurel, "They are wealthy. The Lord will probably tell them to give us a gift for our trip." We did not tell them we needed money. They provided us a place to stay and wonderful fellowship, but no gift. We enjoyed the visit and departed the next morning with the little bit of money we had left over from the $50 received from Laurel's sister. The Lord was not going to send help from where we expected it. He was going to do it His way.

On to Lubbock

Our next stop was Lubbock, Texas. We had dear friends there, and they were expecting us to visit them on our way back home. We drove into Bud and Doe Housour's yard with only a couple dollars in my pocket and a quarter tank of gas in the car. We visited them a couple days and had Thanksgiving dinner with them. I was sure they were going to ask me to speak at a meeting or at church, and I would receive an offering. But they did not. The night before we were to leave, I went into the closet to pray after everyone else had gone to sleep. I reminded the Lord that we needed funds to resume the travel and that He had promised I would not be put to shame. Once again, the Holy Spirit came into the room in such a powerful way and reassured me of His provision to come. Once again, I rejoiced in faith, knowing He was going to provide.

The next morning, Laurel and I loaded our suitcases and got into the car to drive off. We only had the couple dollars and the quarter tank of gas. But we were trusting the Lord. Bud had already left for work, and Doe was saying goodbye. As I put the car into reverse and started to back out of the driveway, she stopped me and said, "Billy, Bud said to give this to you. He thought it might help you out on the trip." She handed me a twenty-dollar bill. I thanked her and told her it would help more than she realized. She had no idea that we were leaving her home with only that twenty dollars and the other two dollars in my pocket.

On to Baton Rouge, Then to South Carolina

As we drove past Dallas, I called a cousin, thinking we could visit with him, but he was on his way out of town. So, we kept driving. Our next stop was Baton Rouge where we were to visit with George and Toya Anding, who were dear friends from my first year in college. When we arrived at their home, I had less than a couple dollars in my pocket and about a quarter tank of gas left in the car.

As we unloaded the suitcases, George said to me, "Billy, I know it's none of my business, but how are your finances on this trip?"

I looked at him and said, "George, the Lord has led us in a very unusual way. I have about two dollars in my pocket and a quarter tank of gas." His face lit up, and he began to praise the Lord with a couple enthusiastic hallelujahs. He proceeded to tell me that he and Toya had been praying for us a couple days before we arrived and that Jesus had spoken to them. With a big smile, George said, "He told us to give you this when you arrived." He then handed me a check that had already been written for 145 dollars.

Laurel and I rejoiced and thanked God for this provision. It was sufficient for the remainder of our journey. It covered the cost of gas, one night in a motel, and food to eat. God was faithful.

We arrived home with a fantastic testimony of how God had led us, how He had spoken to us and provided for us one step at a time along the way. We learned a great lesson in faith and obedience.

Lessons to Consider

I must say here that we don't recommend anyone presumptuously attempt to do what we did. We had a very clear word from God at the time and knew He was leading us. Faith is a response to God's word and to knowing His will and direction in a matter. We are able to act in faith when we know the Lord has spoken or made His will and plan very clear. We should not try to create an adventure in faith by presumptuously attempting to do something foolish. But rather we cultivate our relationship with the Lord Jesus, study His written Word, fellowship with Him in prayer and worship, and be prepared to walk as He leads us. Adventures in faith may be in arenas totally different from the trip Laurel and I made. Since that time, we have had many adventures in our walk with God. We have faced hard times and strange times. We have been on the mountain top and trudged through the valley floor. We have experienced great success and also what seemed to be great failure. But through it all, we maintain our walk with Jesus Christ our Lord and Savior.

The one thing that was so real to me during that trip of faith was the special sense of Jesus' presence with us. The goal is not simply to do great things, but to know Him and His presence. From that special place, we will know the reality of God's word to Jeremiah: *"Call to Me, and I will answer you, and show you great and mighty things, which you do not know"* (Jer. 33:3).

29

Aunt Ider

Hand Pumps and Slop Jars

MY GREAT-AUNT IDA (PRONOUNCED "I-DER") LIVED IN THE house just across the yard from our house. My sister Eva and I were just barely in elementary school, and it was Aunt Ida's job to babysit us while Daddy was farming and Mama was working in Myrtle Beach.

Aunt Ida lived in one very large room of the old house which, as was customary during the first half of the 1900s in the rural South, used to serve as both domicile and business establishment for the family who dwelled there years before. The "house" had four rooms—a family room, a bedroom, a kitchen, and a very large room in front which had served as a general store. Now, oddly enough, the old living quarters served as one of my father's packhouses (a storage barn for crops) while the former one-room general store was home for Aunt Ida.

The old house did not have running water. Consequently, her supply came from an old hand pump stationed just at the back door. There was no bathroom, just an outhouse for use during daylight hours, and a chamber pot under the bed for use during the night. Aunt Ida called it the "slop jar." She would empty the "slop jar" every morning by pouring the contents into the outhouse.

She heated her living area with an old wood heater. Daddy provided stacks of firewood in her back yard to keep the heater going, and I used an axe to split the wood blocks into sizes convenient for her heater.

A Dollar-Fifty Electric Bill

Aunt Ida had electricity but used it as little as possible. When the sun went down, her lights remained off, and she would often sit at the window in the dark until retiring to bed. Consequently, her electric bill was usually about a dollar and a half per month. She would grumble when it occasionally went up to two dollars. It was very common to see her sitting at the window and gazing out as the sun was setting. The photo that accompanies this article shows her at that window and my sister Kay standing outside posing for the camera. Kay was her favorite.

The Electric Fence

Aunt Ida had one very unusual and surprising ability which I now share with you. Daddy had a corn field behind our back yard. At the edge of the field was a hog pen and a mule lot. The mule had been used for plowing before Daddy bought the tractor. But some of the farm help still used the mule even though the tractor was the main source of cultivation. Daddy had only a few hogs. Some he sold, and some he butchered. Hog-killing day was a very busy and very special time at our place. But that is another story. My dad stored the corn in the barn and fed it to the few hogs and to the mule. He would also turn the hogs loose in the field to eat the leaves and stalks after the corn had been picked and removed.

But first he had to install an electric fence around the corn field to keep the hogs from wandering off. I remember one particular day when my father had just completed installing the fence and connecting the electrical power to it. He went to Aunt Ida and said, "Ider, I need to check that fence and make sure the electricity is working properly." Without hesitation, she walked up to the fence, reached out her hand, and grabbed the wire. Then with a quick but easy shake, she pulled her hand from the wire and said, "Okay, Seabrook. The wire is hot."

Some tough women in those days! Her sister, my grandmother Eva (pronounced "Ev-er"), had a bad scar on her hand from grabbing a huge rat and jerking it out of a barrel of chickenfeed. When we worked in the field "suckering bakker" (you friends from Longs know what I'm talking about), she would finish one row and be halfway back down the next before us kids were even halfway down our first rows. With aches and pains, she could still outwork us kids.

O Lord, You are the portion of my inheritance and my cup;
You maintain my lot. (Ps. 16:5)

The lines have fallen to me in pleasant places;
Yes, I have a good inheritance. (Ps. 16:6).

30

Mama

I N THE SOUTH, WE ADDRESS OUR PARENTS AS "DADDY" AND "MAMA." These are terms of endearment and less formal than "Father" and "Mother." Although my father drew close to the Lord in his latter years, my mother, Jessie Lois Long, was always the more spiritually zealous of the two. Mama was not shy about her Christian experience and was always ready to share her testimony or pray for anyone anywhere. Any guest in our home was a captive audience and was prayed for if he or she happened to mention an ailment or problem. Mama once prayed for a visiting insurance agent. He received his healing right there in her living room.

The family's reputation was important to her. She was fearless when it came to sharing her Christian testimony or taking a stand for her faith, and it was important to her that no one in the family do anything that would appear to be a bad testimony or bad example for a professing Christian. I called her one night and told her that our church had a square dance the night before. With a calm but concerned voice, she said, "Whaaaaat? Don't tell nobody!!"

She opened the home for prayer meetings and Bible studies and would invite her friends and neighbors. She was in no hurry for people to leave and would visit as long as anyone desired to stay. Daddy, on the other hand, at some point would get up and walk toward the bedroom, saying, "You all stay and visit as long as you want. I'm going on to sleep." People were saved, healed, and filled with the Holy Spirit in those meetings over the years.

She especially wanted to encourage and befriend any young man who was called into the ministry. I received many phone calls from Mama telling me what a joy it was to get a visit from some neighbor who was now following the Lord or who had stopped in to fellowship around the things of God. She also was my biggest fan and at times made me uncomfortable as she tried to function as my public relations officer, telling folk what a good preacher I was, etc. (When Mama went on to be with the Lord, my sister Eva took over that position).

Mama would often call and give me the latest community update. I did not have to carry on any conversation during these calls. All I had to do was listen and say, "Um humm," every minute or so. I could have laid the phone down, walked over to the refrigerator to get something to drink, and then picked up the phone again without her ever knowing I had left the conversation. Then when she had completed her monologue or was interrupted by some other distraction, she would abruptly say, "Okay. I have to go. Goodbye," and hang up without giving me an opportunity to respond or say goodbye.

I often had to remind her not to drive off so fast after starting the car's engine. I told her she should wait a few seconds because the cats needed time to move out from under the car or off the engine. But every time she started the car, she would immediately press the accelerator and speed off in a flash. We lost a few cats that way, some lying lifeless on the carport, others dropping from the engine as she drove down the highway. She did not do this intentionally. She just kept forgetting to make that pause.

Mama had special mispronunciations for many words. She took us children to "Sinday" school. She gave the kids "Kripsy" Kreme doughnuts. She read the "usepaper" to get the latest "use." As we were approaching Albuquerque, New Mexico, on a trip across the United States, Mama asked me if we were near "Albemarle." I told her the correct pronunciation, and then later she asked me how far it was to "Abbaturkey." She told me she was going to Jonna Faye's salon to get a "primmanent" in her hair.

Mama was a faithful friend. I don't remember her ever holding a grudge. She could get really angry or be offended and insulted by someone and then turn around and show genuine compassion and friendship to that very person. Her desire was to serve the Lord and be a good testimony to her faith and to the Lord. The Bible says regarding the faithful wife, "Her children rise up and call her blessed" (Proverbs 31:28). We also were blessed.

31

The Good Old Days and Wonderful Tomorrow

Driving Grandma to the Dever Field

I WAS TEN YEARS OLD, TALKING WITH MY GRANDMOTHER (MA MA) IN her backyard, when my grandfather (Pa Pa) came walking out the back door. She said to him, "Tharon, I have to do some work down at the Dever field, and I need you to drive me.

The field was a half mile away at the end of a dirt road. Pa Pa did not want to drive her to the field and have to wait on her. Neither did he want to leave her there and have to guess when to go back and get her. He thought for a few seconds, reached into his pocket, took out the car keys, looked at them, looked at the car ... and then looked at me.

"Son," he said, "can you drive a car?"

I was ten years old and had never driven a car, but many times, I had sat in Daddy's pickup truck, going through all the motions of changing gears while pretending to drive it. Without hesitation, I responded, "Yes, sir. I can drive it." I was not about to miss this opportunity.

Without another word, he handed me the keys and went back into the house. I walked around and got into the car and sat in the driver's seat. My feet barely touched the pedals, and I could barely see over the steering wheel and out the front window.

The first miracle was that my grandfather was letting me, a ten-year old boy, drive his car. The second miracle was that my grandmother got into the car with me. From the passenger's side, she looked at me and said, "Son, can you really drive this thing?"

"Yes, ma'am," I said.

The vehicle had a straight stick with clutch, no automatic gears. I put my foot on the clutch and held it down to the floor as I started the engine. I knew nothing would happen while the clutch was down. I put the car into first gear, then gradually let out on the clutch as I lightly pressed the accelerator. The car began to move forward slowly, and I managed to shift into second gear and then into third. I was a happy young fellow, driving the car down that dirt road. We made it safely to the field, and I drove her back home after we finished our work. My cousin Eddie, also ten years old, heard about it and insisted on his turn "at the wheel." Those were the days!

Daddy and Mama in Longs crossroads back in the 50s

My Encounter with the Law

I was twelve years old and already experienced at driving the farm tractor and Daddy's truck around the farm. It was not unusual to see me driving up and down that dirt road with my head barely visible. I had to have a cushion behind my back. In those days, we boys were driving tractors and vehicles when we could barely see over the steering wheel.

On one occasion when we were working at the Dever field, Daddy sent me to the store to get the refreshments. It was time for the traditional nine a.m. Pepsi break that was typical in most southern farm work in those days. I drove the half-mile dirt road back home, parked the truck in our yard, and walked across Highway 9 to Uncle Norwood's and Aunt Venawait's store.

Having purchased drinks and snacks for all the workers, I walked back across the road, got into the pickup, and started my drive back down the dirt road to the Dever field. About halfway down, I discovered that a work gang from the county prison, accompanied by a couple armed guards, were doing some road work. Fearing that the men with the badges would arrest me for driving without a license, I slowed the truck almost to a stop as I tried to figure out what to do. When suddenly one of the officers saw me and motioned for me to approach.

I put the truck in first gear and moved very slowly. When I reached him, he said to me, "Son, is Seabrook Long your father?"

I sheepishly said, "Yes, sir."

The officer then looked me in the eye and said, "Your dad said to tell you to go back to the store and pick up a couple other things for him." I was so relieved. I went back to the store and then waved at the officers as I passed them on my return trip to the field. I'm sure he could barely see my hand and the top of my head as I drove by. So many great memories from childhood, and especially from the small family farm culture of those days. Another *Gone with the Wind*.

The Future

I look back nostalgically at those days. As the old hymn "Precious Memories" says, "Precious memories, how they linger. How they ever flood my soul. In the stillness of the midnight, precious sacred scenes unfold." I have many wonderful memories of events, people, the culture, family, friends, and adventures. However, I know that too many people see their past as a nightmare. But there is one fact that is true for all of us. There is a wonderful future for all of us who know Jesus Christ, the living God.

"Eye has not seen, nor ear heard, Nor have entered into the heart of man the things which God has prepared for those who love Him." (1 Cor. 2:9). Better days are ahead. Jesus said *He* has gone to prepare a place for us so that we may be where He is. He told the thief on the cross, "Today you will be with me in paradise"(Luke 23:43). The promise of Scripture is true.

> The wolf also shall dwell with the lamb,
> The leopard shall lie down with the young goat,
> The calf and the young lion and the fatling together;
> And a little child shall lead them.
> The cow and the bear shall graze;
> Their young ones shall lie down together;
> And the lion shall eat straw like the ox.
> The nursing child shall play by the cobra's hole,
> And the weaned child shall put his hand in the viper's den.
> They shall not hurt nor destroy in all My holy mountain,
> For the earth shall be full of the knowledge of the Lord
> As the waters cover the sea. (Isa. 11:6–9)

It is a blessing if you had a good and pleasant past. But God offers His kingdom peace and joy to you now, and that which lies ahead for God's people is wonderful beyond description. Give your life to Jesus Christ today. Eternity is still ahead.

But meanwhile, the Bible tells us that when the kingdom of God rules, *there will be no breaking in or going out; And there will be no outcry in the streets. And the people whose God is the Lord will be blessed and happy!* (Ps. 144:14–15). We should be praying daily as Jesus taught us, "Thy Kingdom come" (Matt. 6:10 KJV).

32

L.D. and the Religious Folk

L.D. WAS A COLORFUL CHARACTER WHO RAN A COUNTRY STORE A couple miles from Longs crossroads where I grew up. I used to stop in occasionally and sometimes visit with him and any of the local farmers who happened to be standing around the old wood heater that sat in the middle of the one-room store. He watched and listened as people from the local churches dropped in. From his position behind the counter, he would hear all the latest gossip and get a good whiff of all the "dirty laundry" to which he was exposed on an almost daily basis. Consequently, he did not have a favorable impression of many of the church members who passed by. When one of the local pastors tried to talk with him about his need to repent, L.D. quickly responded, "You surely don't want to check behind your members too close. Cause if you do, you're going to be disappointed." L.D. knew all that was going on. He could tell you who had been "on a drunk," who was having an affair, and how the various communities took turns with their episodes at sin.

As you would expect, he never attended church, but like so many people who believe in God but don't claim to be a part of any Christian fellowship, he did have his own philosophy of religion which he was quick to share, especially if he thought you were about to "preach" to him.

He would share his own philosophy of religion with the added implication that you might want to clean your own house before you try to clean his.

He had an amazing insight into human nature, as well as an almost humorous insight into the life he observed around him. He once told me, "It's a shame for a church to have more doors than members. That being the case, if they live long enough, that church will eventually die." Referring to one of the cult groups that came knocking on his door, he said, "The thing that makes me feel so bad is how people treat them. It's about as wrong to mistreat them as it is to believe them."

There came a time when L.D. became very sick and soon learned he was dying. And even then, he had some interesting things to say. Knowing death was imminent he told me, "If I have to take the early bus, that's okay." A local pastor visited him and was telling him he needed to change his life. His response was, "Well, there ain't much sin I can do right now—unless I do it in my mind."

In spite of all this, he did make a commitment to Jesus Christ as Lord while he was in the hospital. A local pastor, Owen Johnson, prayed with him one evening during a visit. I went to visit him shortly after that and found him very eager to tell me about his experience. He told me, "The time was just right. It could have been you or any other preacher, but the time was meant to be. Owen was leaving. He got to the door, stopped, and turned to me. My hand was sort of stretched out toward him. He came back and started leading me in the sinner's prayer. It wasn't planned. It was like two trains colliding. Like lightning striking. It just happened." His encounter with the Lord was real.

Soon afterward, I went again to visit him in the hospital. As I walked up to the door of his room, I overheard a pastor talking with him and telling him that his recent conversion experience was not valid and that he was not saved because he had not been baptized in water and that it had to be by immersion. I thought, *How can this religious leader say something like this to a man who is on his death bed and unable to walk?* I entered the room as the pastor was leaving. L.D. looked up at me from his bed, and the first words out of his mouth were, "That little man was telling me that what me and Mr. Owen did won't but a bunch of sh__. If I won't feeling so bad, we might a had to call 911."

I assured him that the Lord had honored his prayer and his commitment. I told him that normally a believer should be baptized in water out of obedience to the Lord's command, and I personally believe in immersion. However, I reminded him of the thief on the cross next to Jesus. He went to paradise without being baptized. I told L.D. that he was already in right standing with the Lord, that the Lord understood his inability to get out of that sick bed, but if it would help him feel better about it all, I would baptize him by sprinkling right there in that hospital bed. He was delighted. We invited a couple other people to join us, and we had a little ceremony right there. The Lord's presence was with us, and L.D. was at peace.

It is amazing how unloving a religious spirit can be. It is a religious spirit that makes us so rigid, cold, legalistic, unbending, and pharisaical. This type of attitude will not reach our contemporary culture. We who follow the Lord need to "oil our hinges" and "loosen our joints" in order to reach the people in the world around us today. We don't have to throw out our convictions in order to reach sinners, but there are many things we are uncomfortable with that are not sin. We must be careful that our religious convictions are not just religious rather than spiritual. We often separate ourselves into irrelevancy.

Those who desire to be fruitful in reaching this current generation will find themselves being led into strange and religiously uncomfortable territory in the season ahead. Jesus did ask the Father to sanctify us, which is to set us apart from the world. But then Jesus said to the Father, "As You sent Me into the world, I also have sent them into the world" (John 17:18). Sanctification is God taking the world out of us. A religious spirit is us taking ourselves out of the world and separating ourselves into being out of touch, out of reach, and irrelevant to the very people we need to reach. How do we obey Jesus' command to not eat and drink with the drunken while following His example of eating with sinners and being called a drunkard? There is a place where God's love brings wisdom. A religious spirit is so sanctimonious it keeps us away from the very people we need to reach, and when it does not keep us away, it drives them away. Jesus told the Pharisees, "The harlots and sinners will get into heaven before you," (Matt. 21:31, paraphrased). Sometimes we are so busy keeping the outside of the pot clean that we lose touch with the inner living fountain of God's life and love.

33

Fragrance

MY MOM WANTED ME TO DRIVE HER TO THE STORE TO DO SOME shopping. So, I splashed some cologne on my face and went on ahead of her to the car and took my seat. She soon came out of the house and sat in the front seat on the passenger's side and immediately began sniffing the air. I watched as she leaned forward and started checking the bottoms of her shoes. Turning to me, she said, "Billy, check the bottom of your feet and see if you stepped in any dog poop before you got into this car." I went through the motions of checking my shoes, but I knew it was the cologne. I never used that particular brand again.

Smells range from pleasing fragrance to repulsive odor. The sense of smell can strengthen our romantic attraction to someone we love or wonderfully enhance the pleasantness of a room. The sense of smell is vital to our enjoyment of good food but also senses decay and corruption and warns us to discard that which is unfit for consumption. A bad smell can be repulsive to the point of producing nausea. The stench of a rotten egg or a dead rat hidden somewhere in your house is almost unbearable to human nostrils.

Fragrance or odor can indicate if you are clean or need a bath. My Uncle Thomas once said, "By the time you smell yourself, everyone else has been smelling you for three or four days." The smell of your clothes tells people if you are a smoker and reveals where you've been— if you've come from a campfire, a seafood restaurant, a friend's musky house, or a smoke-filled bar. Dogs can detect the presence of venomous snakes by the sense of smell.

The sense of smell can be vivid and strong and have deep effects upon us. I remember smelling the sweet odor of jasmine in bloom when I was a child walking barefoot along the dirt road behind our home. The smell of gardenias still transports me in memory to some of my earliest childhood visits to my Grandpa Willie Long's house and to Aunt Maggie's house next door to his. I remember Grandpa Tharon's old spice and the very intense and wonderful root beer smell that filled the air in Aunt Ida's house when she made tea by boiling the sassafras roots I dug up for her.

The reality of fragrance and our ability to smell are more proofs of God's existence. He is the first and greatest artist. The beauty we see in nature was first in the mind of God. He painted the flowers and gave them their perfume. The numerous fragrances that fill the air, along with brilliant floral colors, bring pleasure to our walk through a nature park profuse with flowers, but they cannot compare to that which awaits us in the age to come. The beauty of heaven's paradise with its wonderful fragrances and sights are incomprehensible to the natural mind and are beyond our human language's ability to describe. God has reserved some wonderful things that we will not experience until we stand in His presence in eternity. There is a God, and there is a paradise, an Eden, a new heaven and a new earth for us to enjoy for eternity.

The Apostle Paul was given a glimpse and said he was not allowed to tell us what he saw and even with permission would still be unable to express it. What we see, hear, smell, and taste in this life is only a glimpse of the panorama and glory to come. This life is only a very brief beginning. Turn your eyes and heart to Jesus. He is the door.

I close with words from the old hymn Ivory Palaces, that was inspired by Psalm 45:8.

> My Lord has garments so wondrous fine.
> And Myrrh their texture fills.
> It's fragrance reached to this heart of mine,
> With joy my being thrills.

34

My Visit to a Philosophy of Religion Class

A GIRL FROM OUR CHURCH IN RALEIGH, NORTH CAROLINA, WAS taking a philosophy of religion class taught by a professor from Duke University. Nancy came to me one evening and shared how she had been brought to tears when some of the other students mocked her for sharing her faith during a class discussion. Nancy was a committed Christian and loved the Lord. She was shocked at the unbelief and skepticism of the professor and the students, and soon came to discuss it with me and fellow believers at church.

Now she was asking me to visit the class. The professor had told the students to invite their pastors to come sit in on the discussions. My first thought was, *This professor wants to pull out all his weapons of complex intellectual, theological, and philosophical thought, all his esoteric terms and make me or any other pastor who shows up look like an idiot in front of the class.* But I knew this was a great opportunity and so agreed to go. The next week, one of the men from the church went with me to the class. I was a little nervous as we took our seats but was filled with faith, knowing the Lord wanted us there.

The professor opened the class, welcomed me and Colin, and then addressed me with the following question: "In light of..."

At this point, he began very eloquently using so many ten-dollar words, rare theological terms and historical names hardly known to the common layman, the meaning of which were very difficult to follow. At first, I thought he was deliberately trying to use classroom esoterica to confuse me so that I would not be able to intelligently answer his question. But then, to my surprise and great delight, he concluded his thoughts with the following question.

"Jesus and the apostles are said to have worked miracles. Therefore, since you teach your people that the Bible is true, what do you say to your parishioners who ask you why we do not see miracles today?"

This professor thought he was dealing with a dispensational cessationist, a person who believes the Bible but also believes miracles have ceased. This cessationist base is a weak position on which to stand in the face of an articulate liberal philosophy which sees it as an illogical and irrational religious hypocrisy. They conclude that if miracles don't happen now, they never did.

My response to this professor shocked him and the whole class. I answered, "We teach that the Bible is true, that Jesus died for our sins, was raised from the dead, and is alive today, and that He has given us His Holy Spirit as His living and active presence with us. Therefore, when people ask me why we do not see miracles today, I tell them, 'Hang around here a while, and you will see one!'"

You could have heard a pin drop as I proceeded to share testimonies of healings and miracles that I and others in our church had either witnessed or been a part of. I gave examples of supernatural healings, exorcisms, and examples of the workings of the Holy Spirit as listed in 1 Corinthians 12.

The same students who had scorned Nancy's testimony before were now sitting there silent and amazed. Suddenly, one of them spoke up, addressing the professor. "The way it looks to me," he said, "you've been talking only theory and words. These guys have been out doing it."

I know there were still some skeptics in the class, but our boldness to share the truth along with real-life examples seemed to embolden those timid souls who secretly believed but who had previously been afraid and too intimidated to speak up.

The professor surprised me as he addressed the class. "This has truly been our most fascinating class yet." He then turned to me and said with a subtle sadness and sense of regret, "I wish you had been my pastor when I was a kid." It seemed to me he was saying, "I am set in my place and position now, and I don't see how I can change now, but if I had heard these things in my younger days, I might have taken a different road."

Certain principles were impressed upon my mind as I left that classroom. I saw very clearly the power of the truth and the reality of the Word of God and how it penetrates the heart when spoken with confidence that comes from the presence of the Holy Spirit who confirms it to the hearers.

I saw the blindness of the world and the emptiness of philosophy. Intellect can be impressive, but devoid of spiritual life, it is so empty. It does not touch the needs and hearts of the common man. I also saw the weakness of silent, impotent Christians who do not speak up. That segment of the class had remained "invisible" when Nancy had been scorned for her belief. But upon hearing our message, they were emboldened to speak up. I also saw the folly of mixture. Some of the students in that class believed some of the Bible, but not all of it. Therefore, they had no real authority on which to base any argument or belief. To be selective with the Bible is to make yourself the authority. Therefore, you have no authority on which to base anything. When human reason is the final authority, we end up with millions of ideas and no real grounds or authority for any of it.

I have witnessed with my own eyes the reality of the Scripture. I have seen people healed through prayer. I have witnessed the miracle of a broken back healed instantly. I have witnessed a young man healed instantly of severe and advanced cases of asthma and emphysema as he was prayed for. I have cast demons out of people and witnessed the same effects as those described in the New Testament.

When given a chance, the Bible will come alive and prove itself true. I, therefore, choose to believe Moses, the apostles, and those saints who have given us the Bible. I prefer to believe the written account of those eyewitnesses who walked with Jesus rather than putting my life and trust into the hands of modern unbelieving philosophers who speak out of their own intellectual arrogance and emptiness.

> [We have] ... so great a salvation, which at the first began to be spoken by the Lord, and was confirmed to us by those who heard Him, God also bearing witness both with signs and wonders, with various miracles, and gifts of the Holy Spirit... (Heb. 2:3–4)

> And with great power the apostles gave witness to the resurrection of the Lord Jesus. (Acts 4:33)

> For we did not follow cunningly devised fables when we made known to you the power and coming of our Lord Jesus Christ, but were eyewitnesses of His majesty. For He received from God the Father honor and glory when such a voice came to Him from the Excellent Glory: "This is My beloved Son, in

whom I am well pleased." And we heard this voice which came from heaven when we were with Him on the holy mountain. And so we have the prophetic word confirmed, which you do well to take heed as a light that shines in a dark place, until the day dawns and the morning star rises in your hearts; knowing this first, that no prophecy of Scripture is of any private interpretation, for prophecy never came by the will of man, but holy men of God spoke as they were moved by the Holy Spirit. (2 Pet. 1:16–21)

Part Four

Warnings

35

Your Sins Will Find You Out

...take note ... and be sure your sin will find you out.

—Numbers 32:23

I see that hand.

ONCE SAW A FELLOW FALLING ASLEEP DURING A COLLEGE LECTURE when I was at ORU. To hide it from the professor, he rested his chin on one hand with his elbow propped on the desk. He held the pen in the other hand and moved it every once in a while to make it appear he was writing. His plan was working until he began falling into a deeper sleep. His head sagged lower and lower until he was sound asleep with his head lying flat on the desk and with his right hand still holding the pen to the notebook and against his head. Every now and then the pen would oscillate as if he were taking notes. Asleep, he thought he was fooling the professor.

The Crow Flies

A seminary professor once told us of an experience he had in a college Latin class. Students had copies of Caesar's *Gallic Wars* written in Latin and were being called on to read and translate paragraphs in class. One fellow was cheating. He had written the English translation in very small fine print just above each Latin word. The professor called on him, and he began reading as if he were translating the Latin. There is one point in the chapter where Caesar sees crows fly over the river. When the student got to this sentence, he continued reading his small, hand-written print and said, "And the *cows* flew over the river." The whole class then burst into laughter. The young man, being puzzled, stopped for a second and then resumed reading, "And the cows flew over the river." Once again, the whole class burst into laughter. Getting very frustrated, the student yelled out, "What is everyone laughing at?" To which the professor responded, "You jackass, you can't even read your own writing! It's 'the *crows* flew over the river.'" His sin was evident to the entire class.

The Sprout Shouts

My father and Uncle Norwood, when they were children in the early 1900s, planted corn by walking down each row in the field, carrying a bag of kernels, poking holes with a stick, and dropping a kernel of corn into each hole. Uncle Norwood knew that the sooner he ran out of corn, the sooner he could leave the field and go play. Assuming he had the perfect plan, he buried a handful of kernels at the end of each row so he could get rid of them quicker. No one would know. But when the corn began to sprout through the soil, my grandfather found large clumps of corn plants growing at the end of many rows. The "sin" that was hidden beneath the soil "shouted" its presence in the light of the sun as seed grew through the soil. The lesson here is that the deed may hide as seed, but the sprout will surely shout.

Here We Are

I read a story in *Readers Digest* years ago about two defendants in court being tried for armed robbery. The prosecutor, addressing a person on the witness stand, said, "You saw two men running out of the store, carrying guns and a large bag of money."

The witness said, "Yes."

The prosecutor then turned toward the people in the courtroom as he again addressed the witness. "Now are these two men in the courtroom today?" Before the eyewitness could respond, both defendants raised their hands.

The lesson in these unrelated stories illustrates the utter foolishness of our attempts to hide who we are. It is not only impossible to hide from God, but neither can we hide from those around us. Who we really are is ultimately revealed in our words, our countenance, and our behavior. We are like the goldfish in the bowl. We cannot run away from home, and there is nowhere to hide. So, it is best to have an honest heart before the Lord, for He loves us and will give grace for reality if we will face it. He does not give grace for pretend. The Apostle John said that if we confess our sin, God is "faithful and just to forgive us our sins and to cleanse us from all unrighteousness" (1 John 1:9). If we walk in the light, we have fellowship with Him and with one another.

> ...all things are naked and open to the eyes of Him to whom we must give an account. (Heb. 4:13)

> He began to say to His disciples first of all, "Beware of the leaven of the Pharisees, which is hypocrisy. For there is nothing covered that will not be revealed, nor hidden that will not be known. Therefore whatever you have spoken in the dark will be heard in the light, and what you have spoken in the ear in inner rooms will be proclaimed on the housetops." (Luke 12:1–3)

36

Lessons from Jonah

THIS CHAPTER CONTAINS SOME VALUABLE INSIGHTS LEARNED from Jonah's disobedience and his attempt to flee from the Lord's presence. From Jonah's life, we see the consequences of trying to run from God. We also see God's persistence in reaching out to us and moving us toward the fulfilment of His purpose in our lives.

The futility of running from God
"Where can I go from your Spirit? Or where can I flee from your presence?...[Wherever I go] You are there." Psalm 139: 7

God's Love for the World

The book of Jonah is a missionary book. It shows God's love for a lost world. Jonah was sent to Nineveh, which was the capital of Assyria, a cruel nation, the nation which was later to carry away captive the northern kingdom of Israel, Ephraim. Nineveh repented at the preaching of Jonah, and God, in His mercy, spared the city.

Presuming upon God's Mercy

Jonah knew about God's mercy ... and strained it to the limit. He knew God would forgive Nineveh (4:2), and he did not want that. He probably assumed God would also forgive him. Therefore, he deliberately disobeyed the Lord and initially refused to go. God's mercy and steadfast love are beyond our comprehension, but in His sovereign wisdom, He still knows how to extend a hand of discipline in moving us toward His purpose. We make a serious mistake when we confuse His love and mercy with permissiveness.

Jonah intended to burn his bridges behind him when he embarked upon that boat to Tarshish. The Mediterranean Sea is very large, and during Solomon's time, ships from Tarshish came to Israel only once every three years. Therefore, it is obvious that Jonah was trying to put himself in a situation in which it would be impossible to change his mind and in which God, even if He should forgive Jonah, would be unable to send him back to Nineveh anytime soon. Jonah probably assumed God would find someone else to send.

Jonah was to learn a hard lesson. If you disobey God, He can forgive you and restore you, but if you deliberately burn your obedience bridges behind you in trying to make obedience impossible, God can still make a way, a very uncomfortable way, for you to get back to where you're supposed to be. A person may think he is "safe" from the will and purpose of God as he sails out onto the blue Mediterranean Sea. But God sends a storm, and then He send a whale. God can get you back to His will by means of "Whale Belly Transport." Many who have tried to run from God have found themselves traveling in a dark "whale belly." Once Jonah got onto the boat there was no easy way out, no easy way back, and no comfortable way back. However, there was a way. He had to marinate in whale belly enzymes for three days. He definitely returned to Israel a lot more tender of heart.

A Whale

A "whale" is a very uncomfortable circumstance which serves as God's means designed to return you to God's will while giving you incentive not to run away again. A "whale" is also a place of second chance.

The Things That God Prepares

The Apostle Paul tells us that all things are for our sakes. God "goes out of His way" to create circumstances that both teach us and move us along toward His will and purpose. Look what God did for Jonah.

> "The Lord sent a great wind." (1:4)
> "The Lord prepared a great fish." (1:17)
> "God prepared a plant." (4:6)
> "God prepared a worm." (4:7)
> "God prepared a vehement east wind." (4:8)

All of these were prepared in order to instruct and motivate Jonah toward the will of God. I'm sure the Lord does the same for us. Wisdom cries out in the streets. The voice and hand of God are everywhere to be heard and seen.

Fleeing the Presence of God

Jonah got onto a boat to Tarshish. Tarshish was located on the most remote part of the Mediterranean Sea, probably in southern Spain near Gibraltar. To sail past this point would be the vast unknown Atlantic Ocean. Jonah intended to go to a location that represented the point farthest from and most opposite to where God was sending him.

He was fleeing not only from the purpose of God but also from the very presence of God. How foolish of us to think we can succeed at this task. It is like a goldfish swimming in a little bowl in your kitchen and deciding to run away from home. There just isn't any place to go. You cannot go anywhere that God isn't. He is there. He "has your number" and your address. You cannot hide when God wants to deal with you (Ps. 139).

Asleep

Usually, a person running from God is unable to sleep very well, especially during a storm. There is no rest for the wicked. But Jonah was able to sleep. He slept to avoid praying. He could not pray as did all the others up on deck who feared for their lives. He was in rebellion and knew what God would say. He was trying to forget what he had already heard. So he avoided calling upon God.

Why was Jonah able to sleep? The Bible speaks of being "at ease in Zion." Being "at ease" speaks of the false sense of security of those who are about to be judged (Amos 6:1, Zech. 1:15, Luke 12:19). Any ease outside of God's will is like relaxing in your house built on sand right over the San Andreas fault just before the big earthquake.

"Throw me into the sea."

Jonah probably saw death as a means of continued disobedience, just another, yet final, step in avoiding Nineveh. He probably assumed he could repent, die, and go on to Abraham's bosom. So he landed in the water to await death by drowning and finally be out of his misery.

Expelled from God's Sight

Jonah "woke up" to realize that he was not dead but in a very dark, remote, and frightening place As the whale descended into the depths, Jonah came to the realization of what it really means to be expelled from God's presence. He had been hurled into the deep like a stone and felt himself falling to the bases of the underwater mountains. The mighty waters covered him with an intense distress.

Sometimes the greatest discipline God can mete out to us is to give us a very excessive and heavy dose of the very thing we seek and ask for in our rebellion. An appropriate judgment upon those who "flee from the presence of the Lord" (Jonah 1:3) is to be "expelled from His sight" (Jonah 2:4).

However, in reality, Jonah was under the discipline of a loving Heavenly Father who had not forsaken him in the least but had let him get a little taste of what he was asking for, while simultaneously working it out for Jonah to get back on the track of obedience.

The wicked mistakenly consider it a relief to get away from God, but to those who in their hearts love Him, it is a most awful terror. It is a cold, hopeless, and most destitute feeling. Jonah cried out in horror, thinking God had actually expelled him from His presence. How relieved he must have been to discover that God still heard his cry. God may sometimes allow Himself to be temporarily out of your sight, but you are never out of His sight.

Jonah learned a few lessons.

1. He had not escaped the presence of God (Ps. 139).

2. He had not escaped the call of God (Rom. 11:29).

3. When you run from God, His incomprehensible mercy and steadfast love will follow you (Ps. 23:6).

4. God's word will follow you and will, in fact, chase you down and overtake you (Zech. 1:6, Prov. 13:13).

5. Sometimes God says, "I want you," and it seems He takes you whether you like it or not (Acts 9).

6. While this was not the case with Jonah, it is possible for people to forfeit their blessing and their usefulness when they persist in stubbornness and long continuance in refusing God (Jer. 7:12–16).

7. When the spirit is willing but the flesh is weak and you are struggling to obey and struggling with your sense of weakness and failure, God's grace is so powerful and His love is so great that if you see Him as your God (Jonah 2:1) and cry out to Him with some inclination to obey, He is able to hold you up, give you grace, and enable you by His sovereign power. (Jude 1:24–25; Heb. 13:20–21).

...God, who has saved us and called us with a holy calling, not according to our works, but according to His own purpose and grace which was given to us in Christ Jesus before time began... (2 Tim. 1:9)

37

Lust and Temptation

Temptation And Lust

DURING TEMPTATION, OUR LUSTS OVERPOWER RATIONALITY AND common sense. We see only the object of our desire. In our temporary blindness, we forget the potential consequences that await us. In those times of temptation, we are not mindful of rewards and plans God has for us, and we fail to consider the horrible consequences our sin will bring upon us. In those moments of overwhelming temptation, we have no props or support other than our relationship with Jesus Christ. Temptation exposes where we really are. When Satan dangles the "apple" in front of you, and at that moment you feel no "glory clouds" or spiritual strength, you must decide whether or not you believe God and whether or not you will obey Him. When temptation is at its greatest, it is the fear of God that keeps a person upright.

Oh ... that they would consider their latter end! (Deut. 32:29)

Lusts are never satisfied.

They grow and strengthen when yielded to. They start out like someone who pretends to be a friend who comes to please you but then becomes the cruel taskmaster who enslaves and controls you. Lust pushes a person to excess. They give a momentary sense of satisfaction and then fire back up with compulsive force. A person who is given over to lust and sin is thereafter controlled and driven by it. He claims to be free to do what he wants to do but is in reality bound and driven by it.

The eyes of man are never satisfied. (Prov. 27:20)

Do you not know that to whom you present yourselves slaves to obey, you are that one's slaves whom you obey, whether of sin leading to death, or of obedience leading to righteousness? But God be thanked that though you were slaves of sin, yet you obeyed from the heart that form of doctrine to which you were delivered. And having been set free from sin, you became slaves of righteousness. (Rom. 6:16–18)

False Promises

Temptation and lust lure and entice us with false promises. They promise pleasure but bring emptiness, disillusionment, and pain. They offer you freedom to do as you please but bring bondage and entrapment. They make you believe that you are in charge and that self is on the throne, but you discover you are a slave to Satan and your own lusts. They promise peace but produce mental confusion, anxiety, and darkness. They promise relief but steal your birthright and blessing. They promise wisdom but lead to foolishness. They promise power, freedom, and spirituality but lead to bondage, corruption, and death.

> Whatever my eyes desired I did not keep from them. I did not withhold my heart from any pleasure ... Therefore I hated life because the work that was done under the sun was distressing to me, for all is vanity and grasping for the wind.
> (Eccl. 2:10, 17)

New Age occult and sorcery promise spiritual light and knowledge but bring poverty, hunger, hardship, gloom, and darkness.

The words of Isaiah say it plainly.

> And when they say to you, "Seek those who are mediums and wizards, who whisper and mutter," should not a people seek their God? Should they seek the dead on behalf of the living? To the law and to the testimony! IF they do not speak according to this word, it is because there is no light in them. They will pass through it hard-pressed and hungry; and it shall happen, when they are hungry, that they will be enraged and curse their king and their God and look upward. Then they will look to the earth, and see trouble and darkness, gloom of anguish; and they will be driven into darkness. (Isa. 8:19–22)

The world, the flesh, and the devil offer nothing but empty promises, lies, loss, and death.

The devil offers his "goodies" up front. He promises to fulfill your desires now but comes back later to collect a heavy price. However, Jesus Christ is the Way, the Truth, and the Life. He is the Living God in Whom we have forgiveness of sin, true, freedom, peace, joy, and eternal life.

Our help is in Christ Jesus.

Jesus told us to watch and pray lest we enter into temptation. He wants us to succeed and to be free in Him.

As a father pities his children, so the Lord pities those who fear Him. For He knows our frame; He remembers that we are dust. (Ps. 103:13–14)

For we do not have a High Priest who cannot sympathize with our weaknesses, but was in all points tempted as we are, yet without sin. Let us therefore come boldly to the throne of grace, that we may obtain mercy and find grace to help in time of need. (Heb. 4:15–16)

No temptation has overtaken you except such as is common to man; but God is faithful, who will not allow you to be tempted beyond what you are able, but with the temptation will also make a way of escape, that you may be able to bear it. (1 Cor. 10:13)

We see Jesus' love and concern for us when in the Lord's prayer He taught us to pray, "*And do not lead us into temptation, but deliver us from the evil one. For Yours is the kingdom and the power and the glory forever. Amen*" (Matt. 6:13).

Our hope and strength are in Jesus. We tap into that help through faith and prayer. Jesus told us to watch and pray lest we enter into temptation. I encourage each of us to take time daily to "enter the prayer closet" and spend time with Him.

38

Lust and Lures

"**D**ESIRE" IS A MORALLY NEUTRAL AND INNOCENT TERM. HOW-
ever, a desire that is strong, ungodly, and evil is called "lust."
Most people associate lust with sex, but it can refer to strong desire for anything. This chapter is written to encourage Christians to be alert
and aware of the enemy's schemes, especially in the area of temptation. The
Apostle Paul said that lusts are deceitful (Eph. 4:22). They lie to you.

Whenever you face temptation, you must remember that you are being lied to. The alluring and attrac-
tive bait hides a trap or noose that
will seize and destroy you.

The photo is not of some sci-
ence fiction Hollywood creation
but is an actual angler fish. The an-
glerfish is a deep-sea fish. It lures its
prey with a glowing appendage
that looks and wiggles like a worm.
A passing fish will be enticed by the

lure, thinking he is about to have dinner, but soon finds he is the dinner.
The victim wants what he sees but steps into something he did not see ...
and did not want.

The writer of Proverbs warns us that the man yielding to sin is going
"as an ox goes to the slaughter, or as a fool to the correction of stocks, till
an arrow struck his liver, as a bird hastens to the snare, he did not know it
would cost him his life" (Prov 7:22–23).

39

Lust and Snares

THE VENUS FLYTRAP IS A BEAUTIFUL FLOWER. THE FLY IS DRAWN TO it by its fruity smell and attractive red color. When the fly touches the stiff hairs on the inside of the plant's hinged leaf...

...it sets off an impulse that causes the trap to snap shut imprisoning the fly. Further movement sets off the digestive process.

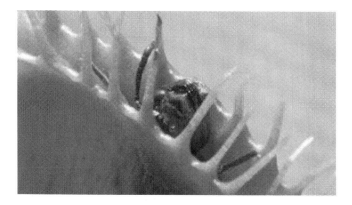

This is a good example of how temptation works. We are lured by what appears to be something pleasing to our flesh, not realizing the deadly snare that awaits us.

The Apostle Paul warns us that our lusts are deceitful. The writer of Proverbs says, *"His own iniquities entrap the wicked man, and he is caught in the cords of his sin" (Prov. 5:22).*

It is important for us to realize the lusts of the flesh deceive us. The tempters that attract us are hiding snares that lie in wait to entrap. Lust has a deceptive allurement appearing sweet like honey but whose end is bitter as wormwood and produces death.

> But each one is tempted when he is drawn away by his own desires and enticed. Then, when desire has conceived, it gives birth to sin; and sin, when it is full-grown, brings forth death. Do not be deceived, my beloved brethren. (James 1:14–16)

The Apostle Paul encourages us with these words:

> No temptation has overtaken you except such as is common to man; but God is faithful, who will not allow you to be tempted beyond what you are able, but with the temptation will also make the way of escape, that you may be able to bear it. (1 Cor. 10:13)

40

Disobey and Have a Party

And they made a calf in those days, offered sacrifices to the idol, and rejoiced in the works of their own hands [the idols].

—Acts 7:41

And he … made a molded calf; … and the people sat down to eat and drink, and rose up to play.

—Exodus 32:4, 6

"It is … the sound of singing I hear." … he saw the calf and the dancing.

—Exodus 32:18-19.

THE ABOVE VERSES SHOW THAT WE CAN DISOBEY THE LORD AND still have a party—at least for a while. One of the problems with human nature is that it so often loses sight of both reward and consequences. When we get caught up in the temptations of the moment or in what we want right now, we forget that there is a reward for faith and obedience and a consequence and reaping for evil and disobedience. And so, like Israel, we make our "golden calves" and have a party.

Moses had gone up the mountain to meet God face to face and to receive the commandments and the laws for Israel's life as a nation. The people became impatient, discontented, perplexed, and maybe bored during the forty-day wait while Moses was on the mountain. They felt that God was taking too long, or maybe Moses was dead. So, they decided to make their own gods. This would liven things up a bit and provide a more cheerful atmosphere. It would help them to feel better. And so, they made an idol and rejoiced before it (Exod. 32:1–6). They were singing, dancing, and feeling good. It actually appeared to be one of their happiest moments since leaving Egypt. Sounds like something wonderful, but what a fleeting deception! Three thousand people died because of this egregious sin.

The enemy of our souls is so very deceptive. He hides in our idols and pretends to offer so much. And we foolishly rejoice in those idols because they indulge our flesh and allow us to do as we please. They help us to feel better by providing a quick, momentary fix. They help us to temporarily drown our fears and to forget our deeply troubling thoughts and unanswered questions. They appeal to our selfishness and our self-centeredness. They appeal to and feed our rebellious nature while keeping us distracted from the one true God.

God calls a person to surrender now and to pay the price of obedience up front. It may mean self-control, waiting, sacrifice, suffering, and doing the right thing when we would rather do something else. The cost is now, but the rewards will surely follow. The blessing follows obedience.

The enemy, on the other hand, offers all the "good stuff" up front. He offers pleasures and "what you want" now. He makes you think it's free or at a discount and with no waiting. As a result, many have eaten at his table, not realizing the horrible price they will inevitably pay. If you think God is asking too much of you now, just wait until the devil comes to collect later.

We must remember that Jesus loves us. Those who follow Him faithfully will reap wonderful rewards. As it is written: "Eye has not seen, nor ear heard, nor have entered into the heart of man the things which God has prepared for those who love Him" (1 Cor. 2:9).

The pleasures of sin are only for a season. The unspeakable gifts of God are for eternity.

Part Five

Personal Integrity

41

Disillusionment: Blinded by Your Limited "Now" Perspective

A CAT WHO SITS ON A HOT STOVE WILL NOT SIT ON A HOT STOVE again, but by the same token, he will never sit on a cold one either. He assumes all stoves will hurt him. This seems to be the way many people respond to bad experiences and bad relationships. They get wounded, hurt, disillusioned, and derailed. Their experience of pain and hurt causes them to be "burnt stones" with distorted perspective, withdrawn, and hobbled by unbelief. This chapter is meant to help us to keep a right perspective.

To have an accurate understanding of truth as God sees it, we must look beyond ourselves and our moment. We must see God's purpose beyond our own comfort and pleasure. True disillusionment means to be free from illusion, but disillusionment with God and Christianity is in itself a delusion. Disillusionment comes from a narrow and self-centered perspective, from making judgments based on ones limited "now" experience and current moment rather than faith in God and His power to fulfill His will and plan. Sometimes He gives us immediate victory and keeps us from harm and trouble, but other times, He may allow us to suffer persecution, adversity, and hardship. Our circumstances may change, but God and His plan remain fixed and inexorably moving forward.

Mark Twain's Mistake

Palestine, before the renewal of Jewish settlement during the late nineteenth-century, was virtually laid waste and its population in acute decline.

Mark Twain visited the Holy Land during that period and, seeing its desolation and the absence of the Jewish state, proclaimed, "See, this proves the Bible is just another book." But had he lived until 1948 and beyond, he would have seen the miraculous rebirth of the nation of Israel and the reappearance of the "land of milk and honey" with the desert blooming. He would have realized what a tragic mistake he made by judging the Bible based on his own limited and short moment in time.

We make the same mistake in our own lives. We become discouraged and disillusioned when we draw conclusions based on our own personal and immediate experience without considering God's overall long-term plan and His sovereign power to fulfill it. There are many periods in history when God's people might have given up had they based their hope in what they saw and experienced at their given moment. We must never assume God has or will fail. Time and patience will always prove God to be true, faithful, and well able to accomplish His purpose.

Examples in Biblical History

As we survey the history of God's people in the Bible, we have the advantage of having the whole story before us. But if we could set ourselves down anywhere into that history, we might experience any number of places where we would be tempted to be overwhelmed with despair and disillusionment. Here are a few examples.

The Bondage in Egypt

You might have been disillusioned had you lived among the suffering Hebrew slaves in Egypt during the 400 years of bondage. You would have been tempted to think God had forgotten you and the whole nation. Living in what seems to be interminable grief and waiting can very easily produce a very negative and wrong theology unless the heart is fixed in God—no matter what.

Time of the Judges

You might have been disillusioned if you had lived in Israel during the time of the judges. After having seen the glorious conquests, order, relative purity, and strength under Joshua, you would now have witnessed a nation of confusion, perversions, and subjugation that occurred on a regular basis throughout that period of Israel's history. Were it not for the recurring emergence of Holy Spirit anointed judges, you might have been tempted to think God had forsaken the nation.

The Divided Kingdom After Solomon's Glory

You might have been disillusioned had you lived through Solomon's glorious reign when Israel was at its height of peace, security, power, wealth, reputation, and prestige and then later to see the kingdom divided into two third-rate nations fighting each other and harassed by their neighbors.

The Captivity

You might have been disillusioned had you lived during the revivals of Hezekiah and Josiah which tantalized hopes of strength and stability, only to see the nation, at Josiah's death, come briefly under Egyptian domination, then under Babylonian bondage, then on to captivity.

The Return

You might have been disillusioned had you been among those who witnessed Israel's deliverance from captivity, expecting her to rise to power as God's people, only to see her rise to a very disappointing stature compared to her former glory and then continue in subjugation to Greek and Roman domination during the 400-year period between the Old and New Testaments.

Jerusalem's Fall

You might have been disillusioned had you known the bustle of Jerusalem and the grandeur of its temple when Jesus walked its streets and yet within a couple generations witness its complete destruction. How disheartening it must have been that within a hundred years of Jesus' first advent the Jews were not even allowed in the city except once a year.

Look at Church history.

The church's history has often been as discouraging as Israel's history. Consider the Dark Ages with its corruption, ignorance, and cruelty. Look at our own contemporary examples. Consider the church splits, broken relationships, moral failures in leadership, foolish behavior, embarrassing antics, and other discouraging situations that have been on display to us and the world.

Our Response

The Bible makes it clear that in spite of Israel's failures and Satan's attempts to destroy them or cause them to stumble, God was able to preserve the nation of Israel and, in the fullness of time, bring forth Jesus Christ our Lord to bring redemption to mankind. Our Sovereign God has and is administrating history and the future to the fulfillment of His plan. His dominion is forever, and His kingdom stands strong, inexorably moving toward the consummation of His eternal purpose. Israel's ups and downs and in and outs never hindered the plan or kingdom of God. The same fact holds true for the Church, for me, and for you.

If we stand faithful to God's Word and ways and persevere with patient endurance in faith and hope, we will ultimately see the rewards that come in God's time. Our experiences may seem inconsistent with what we expected and may vary from one end of the spectrum to the other, from wonderful to painful, from clear insight to the perplexity of looking through the glass dimly. But in all these, we must stand in faith and know that God is God, that He loves us and has a plan for us and for the world, and that His kingdom purpose will be fulfilled. The land may be parched "today" as Mark Twain saw it, but tomorrow it will be a fruitful and fertile land of milk and honey overflowing with the bounty of God's kingdom. And those who say "today" that God has failed will tomorrow look back and see how foolish they were to doubt the Almighty and Wonderful God, our Heavenly Father.

> Why are you cast down, O my soul? And why are you disquieted within me? Hope in God, for I shall yet praise Him
> (Ps. 42:11)

42

Advice to the Woman Looking for a Good Man

T HIS CHAPTER SPEAKS TO A REAL ISSUE IN OUR CULTURE TODAY. The title addresses women, but the message is also for men. Immodesty and sexual license present a great temptation and snare to this generation. It is also a great deception that destroys lives and families. I hope you will read this chapter and share it with those who need to hear it.

Reconsider Modesty

People who are into porn and public nudity often proclaim that the human body is good, and we should not be ashamed to show it. They also charge that Christians, because they believe in modesty, think the sexual aspect of the human body is evil. But to the contrary, Christians frown on public nudity and pornography because sex is sacred, not evil. After all, God created male and female and said, "It is good."

There are two things the Scripture forbids us to flaunt in public—that which is evil and that which is sacred. The evil is forbidden because it is evil. The sacred is to be treasured. It is not for the public eye. It is precious and not to be treated as common. Sex should be reserved for the intimacy of a man and woman in marriage and not displayed as a public spectacle.

God is not an old fogey who sees sex as evil. A reading of Song of Solomon will show that the sexual aspect of marriage is God's gift to mankind. Man did not create sex when God was not looking and then surprise Him with it. Sexual intimacy is a gift God created for procreation and pleasure in marriage. The Bible encourages it but warns of the danger and sin of sexual promiscuity outside of marriage.

We refrain from public nudity because sex is sacred. It should not be treated as common and thus profaned. We should not cheapen that which should be treasured.

Don't "sell yourself cheap."

If you "sell yourself cheap," you will not be treated as valuable. Men subconsciously believe the old saying, "You get what you pay for." If it costs nothing, it must be worth little. The average fellow who has not committed himself to biblical morality will usually fall into the lifestyle governed by the crude maxim, "Why buy the cow when you can get the milk free." So don't sell yourself cheap. Be the priceless treasure you are. Make some guy pay the price for you to be his. A man who is rich in character and integrity will be lavish in his love and commitment to a woman of virtue.

But a man who "buys" what is sold cheap is himself impoverished of character. If you sell yourself cheap, you will attract only the stingy, self-centered, selfish, and immature "buyer." There was a country music song that said, "I like my women a little on the trashy side." It is interesting that he said "women"—and not "wife." The song sends the subconscious message that the promiscuous man is looking for promiscuous women, but his tune changes when he decides he wants a good wife. He then switches to the old Charlie Rich hit, which describes the lady who reserves her sexuality for the sanctity of the marriage bed "behind closed doors" rather than flaunted in public.

Vulnerability attracts predators.

The lion chases the weakest antelope, or the young one straggling at the rear. Predators sense weakness, and human predators sense weakness of character in their prey. So, it is important to develop strength of character. Grow in maturity and wisdom. Put away the childish teen attitude that looks for the "cool" guy. Everywhere I look I see young girls hanging out with boys or men who will probably make a good one-night stand or a short-term romance but who, in the long run, will leave the girl alone, carrying the baggage and weight of the load he irresponsibly leaves behind.

Don't look for the fellow who is following the herd in all the latest looks and attitudes. Find a man who is pursuing a mature future, who will have a job and be able to provide and who can handle responsibility and be faithful to one woman as long as he lives. Don't waste your time with the wrong kind of man. Build a relationship with a person who will be faithful to you and your children for life. "Mr. Cool" is fun for today, but he does not hang around for the long term. Even if he did hang around, you'd find yourself wanting to throw him out.

Like Attracts Like

If you live "in the gutter," you will not attract a mate who "soars in the clouds." People unconsciously gravitate to people who are at the same level as themselves. They identify with and develop relationships with people who are of the same character, spirituality, and lifestyle. If you want a godly husband, you need to be a godly woman (and vice versa).

Sex outside of covenant short-circuits relational intimacy.

If you really want to be intimate, then don't be intimate with a man who has not committed himself to you in the marriage covenant. Real intimacy involves heart to heart communication, personal relationship, and friendship in which a couple really gets to know each other. When a woman's first approach is to give sex to the man, his focus and interest will remain there. He will not be interested in spending the time and energy to know the real person, to be truly intimate at the soul level.

A girl is deceived when she thinks she will catch a good lifetime husband by advertising sex and using it as a lure. The man will settle for the sex and seek it out but fail to press into friendship and really getting to know her. Men are not generally good at communication anyway, and when they are treated to sex outside of marriage, they lose their incentive to communicate at a deeper level.

When he wants to have sex, she feels "used" rather than loved.

Don't sell your birthright for a bowl of stew.

Esau sold his birthright for a bowl of lentil stew (Gen. 25:29–34). He was tired and wanted food. He exchanged what would have been a great treasure and long-term blessing for some temporary relief. He traded his birthright for the pleasure of that which tempted him for the moment. He later regretted it when it was too late. Think of your future spouse as your "birthright," something worth waiting for, something wonderful that God will give you. The pleasures of promiscuity and an immoral lifestyle are like the pot of stew. It is pleasurable for the moment but will leave you empty and alone tomorrow.

Final Thoughts

Find a man who loves the Lord and who has a job or at least a clear plan for his future. Be the virtuous woman of Proverbs 31 and trust God to help you to meet the right person in God's time.

If you think Jesus is asking too much of you now, just wait until the devil comes to collect later. The devil offers his pleasures up front and deceives you into thinking it is easy and free. He gives you a "pot of stew" now and helps you feel better for a moment, but then steals your birthright and leaves you destitute and suffering.

The Lord asks you to do the right thing now, knowing that His blessings and rewards follow the faith and obedience.

Trust the knowledge, wisdom, timing, and love of God. He is right, upright, and good.

43

The Fly in the Ointment

Dead flies putrefy the perfumer's ointment, and cause it to give off a foul odor; So does a little folly to one respected for wisdom and honor.

—Ecclesiastes 10:1

OUR FAILURES OFTEN MAKE A BIGGER "SPLASH" THAN OUR successes. People will often forget all the good a man has done and judge him based on the one mistake or failure in his life. Many contemporary men of God who have done great works and accomplished very significant things for God will be remembered primarily for the sin that was discovered in their lives. A man's folly is more entertaining to the public than his wisdom. His sins will be trumpeted much louder than his accomplishments, especially if they follow his accomplishments.

The enemy would take advantage of our sins and failures in order to produce shame and despair and ultimately to make us quit. But we should humble ourselves before God, surrender to His discipline, and continue in faith and obedience. Our reputations, as well as our lives, are in His hands.

I support church discipline. Individuals cannot grow spiritually unless they face the realities, weaknesses, and sins in their lives. Mercy must be accompanied by truth. But we must remember that everyone has his "dark side," areas where his life is a bit or a lot out of order, areas where he struggles. Every family has its "skeletons in the closet." No matter how much glitter, gold, and iron are on our statue, there are always the "clay feet."

Most of the men of faith we see in scripture would have been disqualified and rejected had today's media been reporting on their lives. Israel had his "Jacob" past. Today's media would have ignored the name (character) change and would have broadcast how Jacob stole his brother's birthright and blessing. They would have pointed out that when Jacob left Laban, his wife had stolen and taken with them Laban's household idols. These items would have been front-page news, and the world would have been looking for someone else to run for Jacob's position as patriarch of the twelve tribes.

Had today's news outlets covered the life of King David, they would have impeached and removed him as king because of his sin with Bathsheba and the death of her husband. He would have been criticized because of his failure as a parent as seen in the rebellion of some of his sons. The world would have ignored God's sovereign choice, David's repentance, and God's discipline in David's life.

The Apostle Paul would have been removed as a candidate for apostleship because of his association with the persecution and imprisonment of Christians and because he had taken part in the martyrdom of the evangelist Stephen.

The world does not forgive past sins and mistakes. It has no mercy on current flaws and weaknesses in the lives of those who labor among us. It takes no account of God's forgiveness toward the seasoned saint who stumbled and recovered. It is unable to understand the changes and transformation in the lives of those who have come to Jesus in sincerity and truth and who have become new creatures in Christ. The "fly in the ointment" has more weight in their minds than the whole bottle of perfectly good ointment currently in hand. The world does not know Jesus and, therefore, is unable to conceive of the inner transformation that comes with the new birth.

Since they are so good at acting and performing, they assume all true spiritual change is only an outward and deceptive façade, a show for the cameras. They have no concept of the fact that God takes an ax to his vineyard to remove those trees that are not His but baptizes His true children in a refining fire.

> Then I went down to the potter's house, and there he was, making something at the wheel. And the vessel that he made

of clay was marred in the hand of the potter; so he made it again into another vessel, as it seemed good to the potter to make. (Jer. 18:3–4)

All of us are marred in the Potter's hands. Our wrinkles and stains are usually hidden from the world around us, and we struggle with and deal with them alone, with family, or with those closest to us. But occasionally the dirty laundry gets hung out on the line for all the world to see. These times require special surrender and obedience before the Lord.

When this happened to King David, he cried out to the Lord in repentance, and he surrendered to God's discipline. When fleeing Jerusalem during Absalom's rebellion, he told the priest, "If the Lord is pleased with me, He will bring me back (to my place), but if He should say, 'I take no delight in him,' let Him do what seems good to Him" (2 Sam. 15:25–26, paraphrased). David did not deny his sin. He did not grasp to hold to what he might possibly have forfeited.

Times of exposure require special honesty, faith, surrender, and renewed commitment to follow Jesus Christ, whether to the mountain of renewed honor or to the valley of humiliation. He is Lord, and we serve Him … not ourselves.

The world rejoices when Christians are "caught with their hands in the cookie jar." I remember some non-Christians gloating in the fact that the televangelist Jim Bakker was caught in questionable behavior and was being sent to prison. My response was to say, "Yes, judgment begins at the house of God. And when He is finished with us, He is coming for you."

> For the time has come for judgment to begin at the house of God; and if it begins with us first, what will be the end of those who do not obey the gospel of God? Now "if the righteous one is scarcely saved, where will the ungodly and sinner appear?" (1 Pet. 4:17–18)

We should not be arrogant against those who might have a "fly in their ointment" if we're failing to swat the swarm in our own kitchen.

> Hypocrite! First remove the plank from your own eye, and then you will see clearly to remove the speck that is in your brother's eye. (Luke 6:42)

44

Waiting for God to Judge

THERE ARE TWO PRINCIPLES THAT HELP THE BELIEVER WALK IN FAITH and show mercy during relational difficulties. The first principle is that God has appointed delegated authorities (both in church and in civil government) to deal with offences. It's easier for a person to forgive an offender when the ecclesiastical or civil authorities are functioning in proper order and meting out judgment.

The second principle is that God is the Righteous Judge. Ultimately, no one gets by with anything, and everyone must give an account to God, both in this life and when they die.

This chapter should encourage those of you who are impatient with God's timing in how He deals with people and who feel the delegated authorities (whether civil or ecclesiastical) have failed to do their job.

God is the Righteous Judge.

Christians often have difficulty with the fact that God seems to delay in punishing those who hurt and offend us. We are glad for Him to be patient and merciful with us but want Him to be quick and severe in rebuking others. We often refuse to forgive offenses because we feel God is too slow in administering justice. We fail to really believe He is the Righteous Judge. We think He is allowing us to suffer while our oppressors get away with impunity. But the Scripture is clear—God deals with people in His own way and in His own time. Jesus was patient in His suffering because He committed Himself to the Father who judges righteously. When we fail to recognize this, we fall prey to anger, bitterness, and unforgiveness. When we really understand that God is the Righteous Judge, we leave room for

God to deal with those who have offended us. "'Vengeance is Mine, I will repay,' says the Lord" (Rom. 12:19). We might add that He will repay when He is ready and in His time.

God is not unjust toward His children.

Job, Jeremiah, and David felt, for a moment, that God was treating them harshly while allowing the wicked to prosper or be at ease. Elihu told Job, "...justice is before Him, and you must wait for Him. And now, because He has not punished in His anger, nor taken notice of folly, therefore, you open your mouth in vain and multiply words without knowledge" (paraphrase of Job 35:14–16).

Job was complaining because it appeared that God was allowing him to suffer while ignoring the foolishness and sin of others. It can be frustrating to experience suffering while it seems the disobedient and foolish are given a "free pass" to ignore God with impunity.

Jeremiah prayed, "Lord, don't let me die while you are being longsuffering and patient with those who oppress me" (Jer. 15:15, paraphrased).

In similar fashion, David prayed, "Behold, the ungodly are at ease, but I have been chastened every morning" (Ps. 73:12, 14, paraphrased). David complained because the wicked seemed to prosper and go unpunished while he, as God's servant, was chastised every day and in the morning, before he even had a chance to do anything bad. However, he gained understanding when he went into the Lord's presence. There he saw the goodness, wisdom, and love of God over his life. He also saw the precariousness of the wicked who are deceptively "at ease" and unaware of their impending and inevitable judgment unless they repent. He therefore tells us not to envy the wicked who prosper. God will deal with them.

We must wait for God to judge in His own time.

When I choose the proper time, I will judge...

—Psalm 75:2

God sends judgment according to His timing after necessary processes are complete. During the interim waiting period, the innocent victim must cleanse his heart of bitterness and unforgiveness and wait patiently for God to act. He must not mistake God's silence as absence or lack of interest. Evil men will give account to God.

> These things you have done, and I kept silent; You thought I was altogether like you; But I will rebuke you, and set them in order before your eyes. (Ps. 50:21)

Let wheat and tares grow until harvest.

Jesus compared the kingdom of heaven to a field where an enemy sowed tares among the wheat. When the servants saw the tares, they asked their master if he wanted them to gather up the tares. He replied, "No, lest while you gather up the tares you also uproot the wheat with them. Let both grow together until the harvest, and at the time of harvest I will ... 'gather together the tares and bind them in bundles to burn them, but gather the wheat into my barn'" (Matt. 13:29–30).

Harvest represents ripening and/or things "coming to a head." One of the weaknesses of human nature is its inability to wait on God. This is especially true in our attitude regarding people we think are deserving of punishment or correction. We must be careful how we remove "tares." Church leadership especially needs to be spiritual, compassionate, and wise in matters of church discipline so that it does not act in an immature and unspiritual way in dealing with offenses and sin in the congregation. To judge prematurely and recklessly is to risk pulling up wheat with the tares. Satan sows the tares in order to destroy. We must be careful not to help him by our impulsive, immature, and unwise reactions.

It takes courage to correct one another and deal with sin in the body of Christ. But it also takes wisdom, love, and maturity for it to be done properly.

Paul rebuked the Corinthian church for failing to pass judgment and deal with sexual immorality in the church (1 Cor. 5) but also exhorted them to forgive and comfort the repentant one lest he be swallowed up with too much sorrow (2 Cor. 2). Jesus commended the church at Ephesus for being diligent to test and judge false prophets but also corrected them because in their zeal to judge, they had left their first love (Rev. 2:2–4). The Church must not indulge and overlook sin, but it must also love and comfort those who repent and seek help. Peter's exhortation speaks of God's love and God's call for obedience.

> The Lord ... is longsuffering toward us, not willing that any should perish but that all should come to repentance."
> (2 Pet. 3:9)

Repentance is necessary to avoid perishing.

Wishing the Fire Were Already Kindled

"I came to send fire on the earth, and how I wish it were already kindled" (Luke 12:49). Jesus was aware of the iniquity and sin about Him. He knew judgment was inevitable and necessary. In sighing and crying over the abominations about us (Ezek. 9:4), we often wish God would "kindle the fire" and deal with the rebellion of man quickly. But like Jesus, we know judgment will come in the proper time. To accomplish the righteousness and purpose of our Heavenly Father, judgment must come in God's way, in God's time, and in the Spirit of God.

When God Arises

When God arises, issues are no longer left to the opinions of individuals. God judges and sentences based on the reality of where people and things actually are in His eyes. That which is of God will be blessed; that which is not of God will be judged. Saul and his house will fall in battle. Eli will drop over dead. The earth will open and swallow Korah and all who are with him. Shemei will face the sword of Benaiah. Alexander the coppersmith will be delivered to Satan to receive his just wages. The plaintiffs, the defendants, and the prosecuting attorneys will all have eloquently stated their cases, but God will arise to judge. All of them will be silenced together as He gives the proper and just verdict. The builders will be dwelling in the structures they have built. Then God will arise, sending the storm to expose the nature of the building material down to the very foundations to test the builder and the building.

When things become muddy, cloudy, and confused, when the enemy is entrenched and embedded in the fabric and seems invulnerable to attempts at being dislodged, when the tares and the wheat grow together and you dare not attempt in the flesh to pull up tares lest you inadvertently injure and pull up wheat, it is at this time that God will arise. He will come and "bring things to a head." The Day of the Lord brings a ripening for harvest—wheat for the barn and for bread and tares for the fire. When God arises, He manifests and approves that which is of God and that which pleases Him. He also manifests, exposes, and judges that which is not of God and that which displeases Him.

45

The Hard Heart

A True Story

MR. C WAS THE ELDERLY PATRIARCH OF HIS FAMILY. HIS WIFE was a godly woman, but he never went to church nor professed to be a Christian (at least not to my knowledge). He was in his mid-eighties and showed no signs of any concern about eternity.

Until he retired, Mr. C ran a small country store beside the highway not far from my childhood home. He was famous for "stretching the truth" by telling some unsuspecting customer that a neighbor had "passed away" that morning. My grandmother once answered the door to find a sad old gentleman standing there giving his condolences regarding my grandfather's death. "Mrs. Eva, I just wanted to tell you how sorry I am to hear about Mr. Tharon's passing." About that time, my grandfather came to the door to greet the startled gentleman.

Mr. C's favorite target was an elderly man named Mr. Faircloth, and occasionally, as people came into the store, Mr. C would tell them that the gentleman had died that day or the day before. When I was a teenager, I was passing by and stopped for a Pepsi. As I walked into the store, Mr. C met me with sad eyes and said, "Son, did you know that old man Faircloth died this morning?"

Without a moment's pause, I responded, "What! Again!" Mr. C shook his head and burst out laughing. I think he was very fond of me after that.

My mother and I visited him one evening when he was in his late eighties and recuperating from a heart attack. "Mr. C," I asked, "when you had your heart attack, did you call the preacher to come pray for you?"

"Hell, no!" he replied emphatically and without hesitation. "I thought I was dying. I called the doctor!" As far as I know, he maintained that disposition right up until the day no doctor could save him, when he stood before God to face eternity.

Mr. C wanted nothing to do with church, and some of his sons followed his example. They were very unusual in their philosophical approach to God. They were neither atheists nor agnostics. They believed in God; they just didn't respect most of the church people they knew. They did, however, on occasion show a subtle appreciation for anyone they perceived to be a genuine Christian. One of his sons asked me to visit and pray for his mother when she was ill. That same son, when dying, was asked if he wanted to give his life to Jesus. He was very serious when he replied, "All my family is in hell. I just as well go be with them." Within a few weeks, he was gone. Facing certain death, he was willing to face an uncertain eternity.

It is a precious thing to have a heart that is soft and responsive to the Holy Spirit. On the other hand, it is so sad how people can allow their hearts to become so hardened that they show no interest in seeking God or knowing Him. It is an awful gamble to enter eternity hoping God grades on a curve or expecting to "get in" because your good outweighs your bad. How can anyone be apathetic, unconcerned, and careless with his eternal soul? There is so much at stake; it seems everyone would at least "turn aside" to see.

The heart also tends to harden when we as Christians continue in our sin while the Holy Spirit and conscience are gently convicting us of our disobedience. We should not think we have a free pass to sin just because God is still using us while we ignore Him. That leads to deception and to a hard heart.

We are like marred vessels in the hands of the Potter. He holds us in the palm of His hand and molds and shapes us as we surrender our hearts to the Holy Spirit, who moves upon us like water over the clay on the Potter's wheel. The Lord knows our frame and understands our tendency to harden and to forget. But He works to soften our hearts as we surrender daily in prayer, obedience, and faith. On a few occasions, Jesus warned the disciples about their hard hearts. But He did not reject them. He worked with them to help them learn, grow, and change. He does the same with us.

> Then I went down to the potter's house, and there he was, making something at the potter's wheel. And the vessel that he made of clay was marred in the hands of the potter; so he made it again into another vessel, as it seemed good to the potter to make. Then the word of the Lord came to me, saying: "O house of Israel, can I not do with you as this potter?" says the Lord. "Look, as the clay is in the potter's hand, so are you in My hand…" (Jer. 18:3–6)

46

Icy Hot

The Lord God has given Me the tongue of the learned, that I should know how to speak a word in season to him who is weary.

—Isaiah 50:4

Icy Hot or Preparation-H

YEARS AGO, A LADY IN MY HOMETOWN WAS SUFFERING FROM that "burning and itching sensation" that we hear about in TV commercials. She sent one of her children to the drugstore to purchase a tube of Preparation-H Ointment, which was placed in the tiny medicine cabinet above her bathroom sink, along with other medicines which promised relief from various physical ailments.

Soon afterwards, her hemorrhoids began to flare up, and the pain drove her back to the medicine cabinet for the relief she so desperately needed. Reaching for the Prep-H Ointment, she inadvertently took the Icy Hot instead. Icy Hot is a wonderful medication for muscular pain and various aches that need penetrating heat, but it was never intended for hemorrhoids. You can imagine what happened as she applied a very generous portion to the afflicted area.

Job's Comforters

Truth, like medicine, is meant to be applied appropriately, especially when we are dealing with people's lives. "Job's Comforters" represent people who are quick to give an opinion based on a superficial observation and without any revelation or true insight into the realities of the person to whom they speak. The first two chapters in the book of Job portray Job as a godly man bearing up under unbearably severe infirmities. Then his friends came and sat with him for a few days. Job probably sensed what they were thinking and knew they were about to open a jar of Icy Hot to rub into his hurting wounds. As a result, he cursed the day he was born. They had come to comfort him but proceeded to add to his distress with their insensitivity, condemning words, and misapplication of truth. How often does this happen in our own lives!

Not in the Same Boat

It is not wise to make rash judgments against people based on outward circumstances. We need wisdom when we reach out to people in their moments of trial so that our words are in season. We cannot tell what season a person is in just by looking at the "color of the leaves on his tree." It is possible for two people to be in similar circumstances for opposite reasons, and it takes revelation to know why a person is where he is. Jonah was in distress because of his disobedience. Job, in contrast, suffered because he was perfect, and God was pleased with him. Jesus was hanging on a cross among thieves and criminals, but he was there for a vastly different reason. Job's Comforters cannot tell the difference; they swing the sword of truth without discerning the people to whom they speak.

What counsel would you give the two men I am about to describe? What would you say to the people who are with them? These two men are in two different boats. The boats are being tossed in a terrible storm at sea. Both men are asleep in their boats while everyone else on board in both situations are terrified that everyone is about to perish. What do you say to these men whose circumstances, in terms of outward description, are almost exactly the same? Well, one of these men is Jonah. He is there because of disobedience and must be thrown overboard. The other is Jesus. He is God and is about to teach His disciples a lesson in faith. A Job's Comforter most likely would have taken his lesson from Jonah, looked at the outward similarities, and would have proceeded to throw Jesus overboard.

Truth and Love

Knowledge alone does not make a person spiritual, wise, or mature. Knowledge alone can produce arrogance and be used to inflict pain. With our knowledge, we need wisdom and insight. And if you feel you are short on these, then just fall back on love. In many cases, compassion, mercy, and love will prevent you from speaking foolishly and behaving unwisely when it comes to giving words and advice that might hurt people. Obviously, there is a time for "open rebuke" and the "wounds of a faithful friend" (Prov. 27:6), but too often people suffer from the insensitivity of a Job's Comforter who brings in the Icy Hot for a pain it was not meant for.

47

Practical Wisdom and Being Led
by the Holy Spirit

A FRIEND OF MINE WAS HAVING TO MAKE A TOUGH DECISION IN an area where there appeared to be some tension between practical wisdom and what the Spirit of the Lord was leading him to do. Below is an email exchange of our conversation.

My Friend's Email

Billy,

I wanted to shoot a quick note your way with an update letting you know that I'm about to take a major leap of faith and leave my current job with no other job lined up to step into. I know many people would consider this to be CRAZY, especially with the current state of the economy, but, at the risk of sounding like a spiritual nut, I truly feel as though it's the direction God is moving me in.

I've been praying for wisdom/clarity of thought in what steps to take next, and I'd be much appreciative for your prayers as well. This is the first time in my life I've stepped away from something without having something else in place to move into ... it's a bit nerve-racking. I'm sure you've experienced those times when you move back and forth between that peace that passes all understanding and the fear of the uncertain ... that's exactly what I'm feeling this past week. Any thoughts or wisdom you care to impart will ALWAYS be welcomed!

Thanks,

Z_____

My Response

Hello, Z_____,

Thanks for the email. I certainly understand where you are. I've had a few similar situations in the past. I remember once, when I was making a similar step of faith, I told everybody I felt like a man standing on a platform blindfolded. I didn't know if I was about to step up or step off. There were times it felt like I did both.

Paradoxes are abundant in our spiritual walk. Natural wisdom and specific, unique direction from the Holy Spirit most of the time flow together without tension. But once in a while, they seem to stand in contrast, at times when the Holy Spirit leads us in what we normally wouldn't do in the practical order of things. Sometimes people will foolishly use the "leading of the Spirit" as an excuse to do some very unwise things. Then other times we use "natural and practical wisdom" as an excuse to not follow the Lord's specific leading because we are either afraid or simply unwilling to obey. We should not use "spirituality" to neglect practical wisdom and prudence, but neither should we use natural wisdom to neglect our spiritual walk. Both are necessary in our walk with God in the real world.

We have to know natural wisdom (which is also godly), and we have to know the voice of the Holy Spirit, who generally leads us into practical wisdom. These are usually in perfect harmony, and we know our instrument is tuned properly when the strings harmonize beautifully. This requires a genuine walk with the Lord and the ability to discern the situation and hear His voice.

Sometimes, though, the Holy Spirit will lead us down an unusual and unexpected path that, on the surface, appears to go against the normal expectations of wisdom. But this is God's prerogative. But it means we really need to know His voice, and not let this principle of the "unusual road" become a stumbling block by using it to cast aside wisdom, discretion, and prudence in the name of the Lord's leading. What it boils down to is that a man has to cast himself at the feet of the Lord with a sincere and honest heart, seeking to do His will, and then put his trust in the Lord for guidance.

I have lived and walked on both sides of the coin. Looking back, I don't know whether everything I did was exactly according to the perfect will and direction of the Holy Spirit or whether the Lord was merciful to me and simply blessed me in times I might have followed the foolishness of youthful or misguided zeal. In any case, however, He has been merciful and good to me, blessing my obedience and showing mercy over my ignorance and failures.

I'll be praying for you, and I know the Lord will direct and guide you. Please let me know how things go. I'd love to hear what God does and some of the lessons you may learn. Keep in mind, if the Lord is in it, it will still require faith once you make the step. A word from God gives you faith to face what comes, but it does not remove the battle or the opposition. It gives you grace to persevere until the purpose of God is done.

Please let me know how things go. I look forward to the next time we can get together and visit in person.

Bless you,

Billy

Usual Advice for the Unusual Decisions

The email exchange quoted above took place a few years ago. I am pleased to say that my friend made the right choice and prospered in his decision.

Generally speaking, it is best to follow practical wisdom as taught in the book of Proverbs. The Holy Spirit's leading is not inconsistent with common sense. However, there are exceptional times when He may lead us in what appears on the surface to be unorthodox and unconventional. During these times, it is important that we ask God to search and purify our hearts. We should also discuss the matter with someone we trust. A person who isolates himself from input is often a person who is seeking to do his own will. We can be led astray by selfish desires and wrong motives, and we need faithful friends who will be honest with us regarding what they see in us. Ultimately, however, we have to make our own decisions. It is important that we be able to walk them out in faith and good conscience.

> Trust in the Lord with all your heart, and lean not on your own understanding; In all your ways acknowledge Him, and He shall direct your paths. (Prov. 3:5–6)

> And when he brings out his own sheep, he goes before them; and the sheep follow him, for they know his voice. (John 10:4)

> The integrity of the upright will guide them… (Prov. 11:3)

> The righteousness of the blameless will direct his way aright, but the wicked will fall by his own wickedness. (Prov. 11:5)

48

Forgiveness

Forgive us our debts as we forgive our debtors.

—Matthew 6:12

ONE BASIC REQUIREMENT FOR SPIRITUAL HEALTH IS FOR-giveness. Conversely, unforgiveness is a major cause of spiritual derailment. It gives Satan an opportunity to take advantage of us (2 Cor. 2:10–11) and makes us vulnerable to the "tormentors" (Matt. 18:34–35). The following paragraphs give some very important lessons on forgiveness.

The biblical command is clear and simple and yet one of the most difficult to obey. A person does not have to be spiritually deep or intellectually brilliant to understand the verses relating to forgiveness, but there is something in human nature that tends to embrace unforgiveness and receives some perverted sense of satisfaction in harboring resentment. "Victims" feel they have a right to be angry and bitter and will go to great lengths to customize Scripture to fit the inclinations of the moment in order to justify their wrong attitudes. And those who do want to be free often struggle for months or years to gain victory. It should not take so long, but the weakness of the flesh and the person's inability to "turn it loose" can prolong the process. But if a person engages the Lord and sincerely seeks His face, he can emerge into freedom and victory.

Understanding God's Forgiveness

Understanding God's forgiveness releases God's love and enables us to forgive others who mistreat us. We forgive because God has forgiven us and commands us to forgive others (Matt. 18:3, Luke 7:47, Matt. 6:12). We often fail to forgive because we fail to recognize the magnitude of the forgiveness we have received from God. Therefore, unforgiveness is often rooted in self-righteousness and ingratitude.

Knowing That God Is the Righteous Judge

People refuse to forgive offenses because they do not have faith in God as the Righteous Judge. Righteous men love justice (freeing the innocent and punishing the guilty) and cry out for it in society. Carnal men, however, confuse revenge with justice. Justice cries out for a man to be dealt with according to truth based on God's law and God's ways. Revenge simply wants to satisfy our lower nature by inflicting pain in return for an injury received. Revenge is indifferent to mercy and to justice. Revenge cares not for God's ways or God's purpose. Revenge is a selfish lack of faith and love. People seek revenge because they do not trust God to be the Righteous Judge. They do not think He will adequately punish their enemies.

We must always remember that God is the Righteous Judge. We are commanded to forgive and leave vengeance to Him.

> Who, when He was reviled, did not revile in return; when He suffered, He did not threaten, but committed Himself to Him who judges righteously… (1 Pet. 2:23)

> Beloved, do not avenge yourselves, but rather give place to [God's] wrath; for it is written, "Vengeance is Mine, I will repay," says the Lord. (Rom. 12:19)

Following Christ's Example and Command

God showed His love toward us in that Christ died for us while we were still sinners and in rebellion (Rom. 5:8). Jesus taught His disciples to love those who mistreat them (Matt. 5:39–49) and to forgive offenses seventy times seven (Matt. 18:21–35). We must forgive even when the offender does not repent.

Forgiveness and Trust

This brings up an important point. Forgiveness and trust are two separate issues. You can forgive someone but still not trust him. If a person apologizes, you can forgive him, but you are not required to trust him unless he repents and changes.

For example: Let's say you are riding in a car with a neighbor who is breaking all the traffic laws, speeding, running red lights, passing on curves, and refusing to yield right of way.

You appeal to him to change his ways, but he refuses to listen to your warnings. Then he wrecks his car and injures you in the accident.

Later, you are standing beside the road with casts on your broken arms and legs, still in pain from your injuries, and your neighbor drives up and stops alongside you. He says, "I am so sorry that I hurt you."

You respond, "I forgive you."

He then opens the car door and says, "Hop in and let's go for a ride."

It would be very acceptable for you to say, "I forgive you and love you because I am a follower of Jesus. I hold no resentment toward you. But I will not get in the car with you again until I know you have changed your ways and attitude about driving and obeying the traffic laws. I forgive you, but I do not yet trust you."

A person who has hurt or oppressed others must realize that forgiveness may come quickly in response to his apology, but he must prove himself to regain trust which has to be earned, and which may take a little time.

A pastor had been in conflict with members of his congregation. He told me, "They have not forgiven me."

"They have forgiven you," I answered, "but they do not yet trust you." I further told him that his apology brought forgiveness, but they must see brokenness (humility and change) before they will trust.

Mercy

Mercy is benevolence, mildness, and tenderness of heart which disposes one to overlook injuries and to treat an offender better than he deserves. It is the disposition that tempers justice and induces an injured person to forgive trespasses and injuries, to forbear punishment, or to inflict less than law or justice will warrant. It acknowledges the offense but wants to help the offender.

Mercy is longsuffering because it desires to bring a person to repentance (2 Pet. 3:7–10) and is a companion of justice. Mercy and compassion will walk with a person to the last mile in trying to help him gain freedom and deliverance. Mercy is given to the repentant. It forgives but follows through with all the requirements of biblical love and integrity. Mercy has strength to speak the truth in love. It forgives the offender while acknowledging the offense and recognizing its harmful effects. Mercy will rebuke and give correction when necessary but will do so in love … and will forgive (Matt. 5:18; Luke 6:35–36).

Conclusion

Forgiveness is so important to our spiritual health. Unforgiveness, however, is an element in the rubble of the past that must be removed in order to build again and move forward with healthy spiritual growth and life. We have a Heavenly Father who loves us and who has forgiven us of all our sins. As we trust Him and follow in obedience in the arena of forgiveness, we will experience anew His grace and strength and the hidden treasures that are ours in His kingdom.

49

Being Genuine

HOW DO WE EXPECT PEOPLE TO ACT WHEN THEY ARE BEING used by the Holy Spirit? A fellow once said to me, "My preacher is so anointed he pure foams at the mouth." That is a strange one, and I am thankful that the Lord does not expect us to do that. So, what style do we use in our presentation?

The Spirit-filled Harvard professor very calmly walks up to someone and, in a very dignified and stolid voice, says, "This is what the Lord is saying to you: 'Your canines will develop acariasis and become acaudal.'"

A backwoods farmer then walks up to the same person and, in a very emotional and energetic manner, says, "Thus saith the Lord: 'Thy dogs-uh will become infested with mites and lose their tails-uh.'"

The fact is these men said the exact same thing, but each one spoke out of his own personality and style. The Lord's word was in the content, while the style represented the individual vessel.

I want to share three examples that show us that we can be ourselves and not have to act a certain, expected way when we are being used by the Holy Spirit.

A Casual Word That Was Supernatural

I was visiting a church in Lexington, Kentucky, a few years ago. The morning worship service had ended, and people were standing around the auditorium, talking and enjoying the fellowship of friends and family. I happened to notice two girls standing on the other side of the auditorium. I was acquainted with one of these girls from a singles conference at which I had recently spoken. I knew that this young lady would one day make some man a good wife, and so I decided to walk over and, in a light-hearted and humorous way, encourage her.

I crossed the auditorium and went up to these two young ladies. As they turned to me, I said, "There is a crazy man out there!"

They both reacted with surprise and said, "What?"

I responded by addressing the unmarried girl with these words: "You are going to make some man a fine wife, and there is a crazy man out there for not having already snatched you up and married you!"

I was expecting her to respond with a laugh, but instead, her eyes filled with tears. I said, "What's wrong? What did I say to make her cry?"

Her friend then explained to me the conversation they were having just before I walked up. The single girl was sad because her fiancé had recently broken off their engagement. She was depressed and questioning herself wondering why he had dumped her. As they stood there, she had asked her friend, "Is something wrong with me that he would not want to marry me?"

The friend had responded, "No. There is nothing wrong with you. He's crazy!"

Then, out of the blue and totally unaware of the situation and their conversation, I walked up and said, "There is a crazy man out there."

I believe I was sent to encourage her. However, I was completely unaware of the significance of what I was saying until the friend explained to me how my words confirmed what she had just said moments before.

I was just simply trying to encourage someone based on what I had seen with my natural eyes. I was not trying to be spiritual or do anything special. The timing, however, made the word supernatural.

A Short Word That Was Supernatural

During our first year of marriage, Laurel and I were part of a church in Southern California. It was composed mostly of young people and had sprung up during the Jesus Movement and the outpouring of the Holy Spirit that was taking place at that time. Multitudes of kids were coming to know the living reality of Jesus Christ and His presence in the working of the Holy Spirit. One thing that stands out in my memory of those days is the hunger for God that was demonstrated in the lives of those kids. They took their Bibles with them almost everywhere, they always had pen and paper to take notes during Bible study, and they all wanted to be used by God in some way.

I remember on one occasion I was about to teach a Bible study to a group of about twenty or thirty of these kids and was silently asking the Lord to confirm my direction for the teaching that night.

Then one of the boys stood up. I knew he was about to share what he thought would be a prophetic word from the Lord. He said, "The Lord wants us to watch and pray." He then paused and stood there silent for a minute, hoping to add something more significant. But that was it. He had nothing else to say, and so he sat down dejected and a little embarrassed, thinking he had failed.

I then stood up. "Our friend has just given a short, simple word telling us to watch and pray. He does not realize how the Lord has just used him. He has not only shared a word to which we should all take heed, but also, without knowing it, he has given a word of confirmation to me. I was just now asking the Lord to confirm the teaching I am about to give. My text for tonight is Matthew 26:41: 'Watch and pray...' My Bible was opened to that verse, and my eyes were on those very words as our friend was saying, 'The Lord wants us to watch and pray.'"

A Miracle of Healing in Response to Hardly a Prayer

As I was leaving a friend's house one day, he and I passed his five-year-old son playing with some toys on the ground. As we discussed other things, the father showed me some sort of bone growth that was on the back of the child's head. It was just a little smaller than half a ping pong ball and had been there for years. The doctors had told him it was nothing to worry about. It would not harm the boy but was simply unattractive and inconvenient. My friend and I did not focus on the child but continued our conversation.

However, as I talked with my friend, I very casually laid my hand on the back of the child's head a couple times, saying, "Lord, bless him." Again, I said, "I know it's nothing to worry about, but Lord bless him anyway," as my friend and I went on with the conversation about other things. Then I drove away feeling guilty that I had not taken time to pray an official and "real" prayer over that child. Instead, I had only said a "Lord, bless him" in passing as I talked about other things.

I was surprised a couple days later when my friend called to tell me that the child's growth had completely disappeared. The Lord had healed it in response to a simple "Bless him" prayer.

So what are the lessons here?

While there are often unusual and strange occurrences during great visitations of God's presence, it is important for us to know that, generally speaking, we can move in the supernatural presence of the Holy Spirit in the normal conversational tone of everyday life. How else can we approach the average person in the world with the reality of Jesus Christ? We can be ourselves; we don't have to act strangely or change our voice. This is one of the keys to moving in the Holy Spirit on the job, in school, on the street, and out in the marketplace. You don't have to walk up to people and shout. You don't have to say, "God-uh" or "Yea, yea, thus saith the Lord." You can be emotional or non-emotional. You can be enthusiastically zealous, or you can be quiet and reserved. The key is to be genuine and real. The supernatural is not what you do, but rather what God Himself does. Sometimes God's work is seen as obviously and patently supernatural. Other times it can be hidden and unnoticed because it is defined by the context and timing and may be significant only to those to whom it is directed.

When we care about people and reach out to them in a real and genuine manner, we will see God at work. And, as in the examples given above, we may find out later that He was at work when we were not aware of it. We may be able to say as Jacob did, "Surely the Lord is in this place, and I did not know it" (Gen. 28:16).

Part Six

Cultural Issues

50

Abortion: Brutality, Loss of Natural Affection, and Child Sacrifice

Part One: The Brutality of Abortion

THIS CHAPTER IS DIVIDED INTO THREE PARTS. PART ONE IS CALLED "The Brutality of Abortion." Part Two is called "The Absence of Natural Affection." Part Three is called "Abortion is legalized child sacrifice." I included this topic because of the seriousness of the issue and because of the law recently enacted in New York allowing babies to be aborted even during the third trimester, which would be right up until the time of birth. This law also allows them to kill the child if the aborted baby is born alive. This is a cruel and wicked abomination. It is these practices that will bring the judgment of God upon our nation. It is time for Christians to pray and for pastors to speak up in the pulpits.

Bodies in Jars

Excavations of pre-Israel Canaan uncovered many jars containing the remains of children sacrificed to Baal. Other excavations discovered many jars containing the remains of infants who had been sacrificed to Baal during King Ahab's time. These jars bring to mind the photos of garbage cans filled with baby parts at abortion clinics. I showed one of these pictures to a high school girl once. Her reply was, "That's just propaganda." She was not able to bring herself to face the fact she was looking at actual babies dismembered and thrown away. Her political position would not allow her to accept the fact that these babies went through torture and excruciating pain as they were being killed and taken from their mother's wombs.

The religious rites of Baal worship were noted for their sexual and immoral indulgences and for child sacrifice. Our own culture, with its rampant sexual promiscuity, has produced over sixty million abortions. The sexual practices of Baal worship and the promiscuity of our own current culture show that unbridled sexual activity outside of marriage leads to the death of children, whether sacrificed in religious worship to a pagan god or dismembered inside a mother's womb to the god of convenience. In either case, the remains of infants are left behind in jars and garbage bins.

Statistics show that a large percentage of women/girls who are allowed to see the ultrasound of their baby will choose not to go through with the abortion. They see a child in the womb and not a blob or mass of cells. That's why the abortion industry lobbies so hard to block any legislation that requires them to show the ultrasound to the mother. The child in the womb recoils in pain from the sharp instruments of the abortionist. One well-known video showing the ultrasound of an abortion was appropriately titled "The Silent Scream." If the same procedures were performed on a baby outside the womb, the cries of that same child would be heartwrenching.

The practice of partial-birth abortions proves the evil and callousness of the industry. It is absolutely astounding that any normal adult would not grieve and be repulsed at the idea of partial-birth abortions. In this practice, the live child is first pulled from the womb and into the birth canal, except for the head. The abortionist then punctures the base of the skull, suctions out the brains and removes a dead baby from the mother's body. If the entire body of the child were to be removed first, this practice would legally be considered murder. It is foolishness to say that location determines life. The practice of partial-birth abortions proves that the debate over when life begins is a waste of time when dealing with avid abortionists. The evidence seems to show they do not really care.

Our culture has degenerated to the point that sexual promiscuity is prevalent, encouraged, and expected. In this atmosphere, there will be growing numbers of unplanned and unwanted pregnancies. The operative word is "unwanted." Abortions are given not for medical reasons but rather for the convenience of the mother and because of economic factors in her life. The mother does not want the child, and the abortion industry is making millions and millions of dollars.

Murder, whether it is on the street or in the womb, causes the land to be defiled and "guilty of blood" (Deut. 21:6–9; Num. 35:33–34). The moral issues do matter. A godly and righteous nation might survive even with bad economic policies, but an immoral nation filled with ungodly practices will inevitably face the judgments of God, unless there is repentance. Where are the cries from the church and from the pulpit?(

We are fearfully and wonderfully made. It is in the womb that God first breathes life into a person. We should stand in awe and reverence at this divine and mysterious process. We should also be afraid to trample upon that which is so sacred and wonderful.

Rulers and legislators should take note. God is the Righteous Judge, and all men must give an account to Him. This applies to those who make the laws.

> Shall the throne of iniquity, which devises evil by law,
> Have fellowship with You?
> They gather together against the life of the righteous,
> And condemn innocent blood." (Ps. 94:20–21)

Who is more innocent than the babies in the womb?

Part Two: The Absence of Natural Affection

"With Child"

It is not insignificant that the Bible translators in the Old and New Testaments translated the Hebrew and Greek terms for pregnancy as being "with child." The babe in the womb is a child ... not a mass of tissue. The Bible says that Mary's cousin Elizabeth, who was six months pregnant, had conceived a *son*. It was a son ... not a blob of tissue. John the Baptist was filled with the Holy Spirit, even as a babe, in his mother's womb. Elizabeth, when she heard Mary's greeting, was also filled with the Holy Spirit, and the babe John leaped within her womb. He was a person even before birth, and he supernaturally responded to the presence of the Son of God in Mary's womb (Luke 1:15, 36, 44; Matt. 1:18; Matt 1:23).

God is the Father of spirits. Human procreation produces a physical body, but the real person is the human spirit that God creates and breathes into us when we are conceived. Psalm 139 reveals that our spirits, along with God's plan and purpose, are given to us even before we are born. The Lord forms our inward parts (our spirits) and covers us in the womb. The psalmist tells us that God "sees our substance, being yet unformed. And all the days fashioned for us were written in His book when as yet there were none of them" (Psalm 139:6). We are trampling on sacred ground when we assault the babe in the womb. It is God's nursery, a place where He is at work (Eccl. 3:20, 12:7; Ps. 139).

Jesus clearly manifested His love for little children when they brought them to Him. He took them up in His arms, laid His hands upon them, and blessed them. He also gave a stern warning. "Whoever causes one of these little ones who believe in Me to stumble, it would be better for him if a millstone were hung around his neck, and he were thrown into the sea" (Mark 9:42). These sobering words should cause us to stand in the fear of God regarding how we treat them, even in the womb.

Lacking Natural Affection

One of the characteristics of the latter days is that men and women will lack natural affection. A people who forsake the Lord will at best become callous and indifferent and at worse brutal, cruel, and barbaric. These adjectives describe abortion at any phase of pregnancy. How can killing a baby after it is born be anything but selfish, cruel, and brutal? A child is tortured and killed at any phase of pregnancy. It goes against nature to blind our eyes to this disgraceful procedure (2 Tim. 3:1–3; Rom. 1:31).

Cruel

A society without God can be cruel, heartless, unfeeling, and sadistic with no love for family or neighbor and no compassion or sympathy for the suffering. The nation that can kill babies will eventually progress to euthanasia, killing the infirm and the elderly. A friend of mine once said, "The generation that approved and legalized abortion may be the generation that will themselves be the first victims of the nation's approval of euthanasia," which will lead to the killing of any person or group that society deems unworthy to live (Deut. 28:50).

The Apostle Paul uses the word "perilous" to describe the latter days (2 Tim. 3:1–3). This same word is translated "fierce" in describing the Gadarene demoniac who was wild in the tombs, cutting himself and breaking chains (Matt. 8:28). There are many historical examples that show the Apostle Paul was correct in his description of man's potential for evil.

The Nazis in World War II slew babies along with innocent men, women, and children in their prison death camps. Then, when the war ended, Stalin allowed his soldiers and the civilian mobs in areas of Eastern Europe occupied by the communists to kill innocent men, women, and children of German descent. These were innocent citizens who just happened to have German ancestry. The Eastern European reprisals after the war were as bad as the murders that took place in the Nazi SS camps during the war. A documentary on the post-war slaughter that occurred is titled *The Savage Peace*.

King Herod, being threatened by the birth of Jesus, sent his soldiers to Bethlehem to put to death all the male babies from newborn up to two years old. There are groups in our society today who advocate similar practice but in the respectable cover of the medical profession.

These examples show the potential degeneration and descent into cold, hard evil that any society is capable of when it starts down the slippery slope. Who knows how far this process will go in finding victims, and where will it stop? Without God, the heart can harden and grow in its beast-like propensities. Unless cultivated by an intimate relationship with Jesus through prayer and the written Word of God, the Christian's heart tends to harden. But an unbelieving person who does not know God and who despises His Word has the potential to harden his heart, lose natural affection, and tolerate practices that are unspeakably callous. Governed by self-interest, selfishness, and self-centeredness, people become desensitized to the pain and needs of others, and in arrogance and rebellion, they become tools of the devil. This type of society tends to follow the Apostle Paul's description of the progressive slide from passive complacency to the arrogant display and bold presentation of sin in its fullness. Abortion has progressed (or rather degenerated) from initially killing what they claimed was "only a blob of tissue" to the current brazen and shameless proposal to kill the baby at birth and even after birth. This is one mark of a society moving toward the "fullness of iniquity" referred to in the Bible.

The Fullness of Iniquity

Biblical examples show us that God sends judgment when iniquity reaches its fullness. At that point, the judgment of God is inevitable ... unless there is nationwide repentance. The acceptance and approval of child sacrifice are among the abominations that will precipitate that judgment. When Israel entered the promised land, the iniquity of Canaan had reached its fullness. It was filled with every type of abomination, including child sacrifice. Leviticus 18:25 says, "For the land is defiled; therefore I visit the punishment of its iniquity upon it, and the land vomits out its inhabitants."

My guess is that unless there is repentance on a national scale, the judgment of God will fall on our nation for killing over sixty-five million babies in and out of the womb. The practice will then stop … but at great cost.

> "For behold, the day is coming, burning like an oven. And all the proud, yes, all who do wickedly will be stubble. And the day which is coming shall burn them up," says the Lord of hosts. (Mal. 4:1)

> For the day of the Lord is great and very terrible; who can endure it? (Joel 2:11)

> Who shall not fear You, O Lord, and glorify Your name? For You alone are holy. For all nations shall come and worship before You, for Your judgments have been manifested. (Rev. 15:4)

Part Three: Abortion is legalized child sacrifice.

Woe to those who decree unrighteous decrees…

—Isaiah 10:1

Child Sacrifice

It is very strange that lawmakers were laughing and celebrating a law that allows them to kill babies even at birth. Abortion is a tragedy at any stage, but this new law exposes the real heart of the abortion industry and those who support it. They obviously don't care when life begins. Everyone knows a child born in the ninth month is *obviously* alive and is a person. This amounts to child sacrifice and is a blatant disregard for God and His

Word. The Lord spoke through Ezekiel the prophet, saying, "You have slain My children" (Ezek. 16:21). He is not indifferent to these deaths.

Almighty God, Creator of the heavens and the earth, and the Righteous Judge of all mankind calls it an abomination. He places the practice alongside witchcraft and the occult. The land is polluted by the shedding of innocent blood. God sets His face against those who practice it and gives a stern warning to those who close their eyes and ignore it. The nation is accountable for the abomination, and the Church is accountable for its apathy and silence and for not speaking up. The blood is also on the hands of ministers and pastors who have endorsed it or who, in the fear of man, have remained silent in the pulpit.

> For after they had slain their children for their idols, on the same day they came into My sanctuary to profane it; and indeed thus they have done in the midst of My house. (Ezek. 23:39)

> And if the people of the land should in any way hide their eyes from the man, when he gives some of his descendants to Molech [offer his children in the fire], ... I will set my face against that man and against his family. (Lev. 20:4−5)

We must remember that surely God will judge an unrepentant nation for the death of innocent children. But we must also remember that judgment begins at the house of God, and it starts with the leaders.

Secular rulers will answer to God.

The blood of innocent babies cries out to God against government officials who enact laws permitting and supporting abortion. People generally expect spiritual leaders to be accountable to God. But secular rulers and legislators are not excluded. They will ultimately answer to God for the laws on which they place their name and stamp of approval. Individuals in legislative bodies mistakenly think they are hidden in the anonymity of the group, and they fall into the snare of thinking they are not personally accountable to God for the laws they make. But there is no such thing as anonymity. God not only sees "all" but also sees "each" ... and takes notes. He watches the halls of government, whether church or state. Leaders are commanded to rule in the fear of God, knowing He has placed them in their positions, and that He will come to judge the judges.

Leaders Who Despise God's Word

> ...because they had not executed My judgments, but had despised My statues ... Therefore, I also gave them up to statutes that were not good, and judgments by which they could not live ... For when you ... make your sons pass through the fire [child sacrifice], you defile yourselves with all your idols.
>
> —Ezekiel 20:24–25, 31

Leaders who do not fear God will be given up to laws that are not good, laws that are perverse and based on the imaginations of their own heart. Such men will be controlled by selfish ambition and evil motives, creating a government that is corrupt, rife with lies, and given over to error, abuse, and hypocrisy (Isa. 19:13–14).

When God is despised, the nation and its rulers become not only corrupt but also foolish. One minister said, "Man without God is insane." We see this in the schizophrenic nature of our own legal system. One law based on divine order and respect for parental authority does not allow a school teacher to give an aspirin to a child without parental consent and permission, while another law completely disregards moral law and allows doctors to give abortions to minor children without notifying the parents.

Tophet

The bodies of children sacrificed in the fire were buried in a place called Tophet. Jeremiah proclaimed that because they had filled this place with the blood of the innocents, God was going to send judgment and cause them to fall before the sword of their enemies. The burial place would not have room for all the bodies, and its name would be changed from Tophet to the Valley of Slaughter.

> And they caused their sons and daughters to pass through the fire, practiced witchcraft and soothsaying, and sold themselves to do evil in the sight of the lord, to provoke Him to

anger. Therefore the Lord was very angry with Israel, and removed them from His sight; there was none left but the tribe of Judah alone. (2 Kgs. 17:17–18)

Righteousness exalts a nation. Sin brings judgment, decline, and downfall. God will bring every work into judgment. The slaughter of over sixty-five million infants will not go unpunished, unless there is repentance on a national scale. Those who sigh and cry because of the abominations should be fasting and praying and calling on God.

Then I saw a great white throne and Him who sat on it, from whose face the earth and the heaven fled away. And there was found no place for them. And I saw the dead, small and great, standing before God, and the books were opened. And another book was opened, which is the Book of Life. And the dead were judged according to their works, by the things which were written in the books. (Rev. 20:11–12)

May the Lord have mercy on our nation. May we repent before judgment becomes inevitable.

51

God and Creation

A THEISTIC HUMAN PHILOSOPHY IS AN EXERCISE IN IGNORANT arrogance, not recognizing the possibility that mankind lives in a limited, finite, created realm from which he has no means or capacity to comprehend the infinite realities outside of that realm—unless he enters a relationship with the Creator Himself. Trying to find meaning and answers apart from God is like bringing a lamp to a sundial to find the time.

No matter what your religion or spiritual belief system is, it logically must bring you to the intellectual and philosophical conclusion that there has to be a creator and a sovereign manager over it all. For instance, reincarnation is a complicated process, if it were true. If you believe in reincarnation, I will have to ask you, "Who manages and directs it? Where did the spirits come from that keep reincarnating upward? Who does the evaluating regarding good and bad and which ones move upward and which ones move downward?" You always come back to the necessity of a creator and manager. Even the dynamics of pantheism that pervades eastern religions and the New Age movement require the existence of an all-powerful, higher power to create and manage the processes. Therefore, all religions bring you back to the need for a personal God who created and manages His creation.

What about the secular humanist and atheist? Even if you believe in evolution, you still end up with "how did it all get started?" All the known elements of "creation," the laws of nature, laws of the universe, down to the complex systems in the human body and human consciousness had to have a starting point. They did not create themselves into being. Creation itself shouts the existence of a creator, and its orderly perpetuation and smooth functioning shout the existence of a higher power who manages it all. Such magnitude of reality and complexity requires a manager or administrator.

Like the unbelieving scientist and philosopher, I cannot comprehend eternity past. How can God exist eternally past? I can logically understand eternity future, but the past is impossible to understand. But I resolve that question by looking at the present. The overwhelming evidence of God Almighty are clear and plain when you look at all the systems in the human body, when you look at the order and precision in the universe, when you look at the glory of nature and the beauty of flowers. The following paragraphs give logical evidence of the reality of the God of the Bible. That's why Christianity and the Bible are my logical and only choice.

Life is infinitely too complex to have come into being randomly and by itself. There are so many interdependent systems that are necessary for the existence of life on earth, and the degree of refinement, accuracy, and perfection in the coordinated performance of all these operations necessary for life are too complex to exist apart from design. They are independent yet dependent and interdependent, and their functions must be exactly precise and with perfect timing. These dynamics testify to intelligent design; that is the existence and reality of God. Even evolutionists betray an inward sense of the need for a designer when they constantly treat "evolution" as a god as if it perceives, designs, and creates. How can nature—with no consciousness, sight, or thinking power—decide that a lizard or insect or snake should be colored so that it can camouflage itself for survival.

I see the reality of God in many simple, subtle, and yet so obvious aspects of life that we often take for granted. For example, look at your nose. It is located in a most beneficial and practical place on your body. The nostrils point down, so you don't have to cover them to keep rain from falling into your sinuses. It is just above your mouth so that the sense of smell can work together with your sense of taste to help you enjoy your food. I can think of other more unpleasant places where your nose could have been located. Your ears have their own little "satellite dishes" on the sides of your head to help capture sound. Your eyes are in recessed sockets to help protect them. They are located in the front of your head so you can see where you are going. Your feet point in the same direction as your eyes. The size of our moon, its distance from the earth, the tilt of the earth's axis, the distance of the earth from the sun—if you change any of these in the smallest degree, you will end life on earth. This is also true of the numerous systems that operate in the human body: skeletal, digestive, circulatory, reproductive, pulmonary, muscular, neurological, etc. How do you account for human consciousness and self-awareness? Your own consciousness is a mystery beyond the physical parts of the body and cannot be explained by brain cells alone.

Life is just too orderly and complex to have come into being without design. Everywhere you look you see evidence of design. The necessary interacting, interdependent, and coordinated operations of the systems required for life, from biological to geological to astronomical, are so exact and precise that it is impossible for life to have developed on its own by chance.

And what about sex? I could rest my case on that point but will continue my thoughts. Male and female. In terms of species development, the world could not have seen reproduction without the complete and fully developed male and female. If you could have reproduction without these, then there would have been no need for male and female. So how could this have possibly evolved—two separate systems made to be completely separate and absolutely compatible and yet totally interdependent with neither being able to carry out the reproductive function without the other? There would have been no births, no reproduction without fully developed reproductive systems. "*Somebody*" had to design this, and it had to begin fully functional.

This law of "irreducible minimums" eliminates the possibility of evolution. Scientists have discovered that there is no such thing as a "simple cell" to start with. (Just get a scientist to explain the complexity of the DNA in any single cell.) I recently saw a documentary on TV in which a scientist described the complexity even in the single-celled amoeba. Too many complex, separate yet interdependent systems have to be in operation at the same time for life to exist. If you eliminate any one of them, life will cease to exist. In other words, for life to exist, all of these systems would have to be created simultaneously.

Evolution is a very awkward and yet convenient way for people to try to avoid God. Evolution itself is foolish, but if you do away with God, evolution is about the only thing you are left with to explain how we got here. So the very concept of "evolution" is a product of intellectual "devolution," i.e., what you arrive at by default when you reject the reality of God. A few years ago, I was reading a book in which the author had recorded his conversation with a prominent evolutionist. The evolutionist told him, "We did not evolve from anything. Life is too complex to have evolved, but I prefer to believe in evolution than to believe in God."

I prefer to believe in God. It is more comforting to believe in God, that there is a power beyond and greater than our comprehension, who created us as finite beings with limited capacity to understand the created universe and who created us with no capacity within ourselves to comprehend or grasp the infinite realities beyond our created universe, but who also desires to introduce us to Himself and take us beyond what we see and know. As the Bible says, "Eye has not seen, nor ear heard, nor have entered into the heart of man the things that God has prepared for those who love Him" (1 Corinthians 2:9).

If there is no God, then we face the most depressing prospects, a meaningless procession of people heading into an eternal oblivion, nothing above and nothing beyond. But there is a God, and this gives us hope for eternal life. The very issues raised in the paragraphs above echo the words of the psalmist who tells us that the heavens, the earth, and all creation testify to the glory and existence of God. This means there is more to life than this life. This is only the beginning, not the end. To see and understand this, one must look up to the One who is the beginning and the end, the Alpha and Omega, our Heavenly Father and Jesus Christ our Lord who brings us to the Father.

> The heavens declare the glory of God; and the firmament shows His handiwork. Day unto day utters speech, and night unto night reveals knowledge. There is no speech nor language where their voice is not heard. Their line has gone out through all the earth, and their words to the end of the world (Ps. 19:1–4). For since the creation of the world His invisible attributes are clearly seen, being understood by the things that are made, even His eternal power and Godhead. (Rom. 1:20).

> For by Him all things were created that are in heaven and that are on earth, visible and invisible, whether thrones or dominions or principalities or powers. All things were created through Him and for Him. (Col. 1:16)

> For of Him and through Him and to Him are all things, to whom be glory forever. Amen. (Rom. 11:36)

In the beginning God created the heavens and the earth.
(Gen. 1:1)

52

Calling Evil Good and Good Evil

The wicked prowl on every side, when vileness is exalted among the sons of men.

—Psalm 12:8

Woe to those who call evil good and good evil; Who put darkness for light, and light for darkness.

—Isaiah 5:20

B ACK IN 1977, IT WAS VERY COMMON IN OUR CULTURE TO CALL evil good. Immoralities of various sorts were glorified on TV and in the movies. They still are. But evil left unchecked in a society will grow toward its fullness. I remember speaking in one of our home fellowship meetings at that time (1977) and saying, "We are seeing people call evil good. Immorality is glorified as normal. However, in the coming years, we will see a progression of evil. The next step in the degeneration of our society will be to call good evil." That trend is now applicable in our cultural mindset today. Evil is being treated as good, and good is being treated as evil. Christianity used to be respected, even by those who did not practice it. Now it is treated as a liability in many aspects of our culture. For example, presidential appointees who are outspoken Christians have found it a disadvantage in the congressional confirmation process. Godly people are viewed with reproach while various immoral lifestyles are honored and praised.

There are growing forces in our nation that seek to remove God and biblical Christianity from our culture. These forces "preach" against intolerance and hate while exhibiting these very attitudes towards Christians. A culture that calls evil good and good evil will eventually persecute Christians with the same intensity we have witnessed in other nations. As our culture lays aside biblical values and removes God from its institutions, government, and education, it will begin more and more to despise Christians and hate them because of their commitment to Jesus Christ as the only way to God and because of their stand on moral issues as taught in the Bible. During the Roman persecutions, Christians were called "haters of mankind" because of their disapproval of and refusal to participate in cultural immoralities prevalent at the time. There are forces in our culture now moving in that same direction. Just as the devil has historically created an irrational and unreasonable hatred toward the Jews, which we are witnessing today, he will also stir up and fuel the same unreasonable and intense hatred toward those who follow Jesus and stand on the Bible as the Word of God.

Calling evil good and good evil is one of the indicators of iniquity reaching its fullness. God judges a nation when iniquity reaches its fullness. God sent Noah's flood because "the Lord saw that the wickedness of man was great in the earth" (Gen. 6:5). God sent fire and brimstone upon Sodom and Gomorrah because the sin had reached its fullness (Gen. 19:13). In His covenant with Abraham, the Lord told him that his descendants would enter and possess the land when the iniquity of the Canaanites had reached its fullness (Gen. 15:13–16). Moses warned the Israelites to not adopt and practice the various abominations that were prevalent in Canaan, lest the land vomit them out as it was vomiting out the pagans whom they dispossessed. Israel's entrance into the land fulfilled God's promise to Abraham and fulfilled God's word that Israel's entrance would be the judgment of God on the abominations that were prevalent in the land. We should take note that the Apostle Paul warns us that the wrath of God will be upon those who are given over to their sin and who are filled with the fullness of iniquity while refusing to repent. He also warns those who place approval on and honor those who practice these abominations (Rom. 1:18–32). The wicked prowl on every side when vileness is exalted among the sons of men.

So what are Christians to do in this atmosphere? Here are a few suggestions.

We should faithfully proclaim the gospel and remember that Christ died on the cross because He loves the world and wants to reconcile them to Himself.

The Church and its ministers should be calling the nation to repent. Jonah proclaimed to Nineveh that they must repent or be overthrown in forty days. The whole city responded to Jonah's message of repentance, and God spared the city. I believe God is going to pour out His Holy Spirit upon our nation. If the nation repents of its abominations, we will see a great visitation of God upon the whole land. But if there is no national repentance, the Holy Spirit will fall upon the Church while inevitable judgment falls upon the nation.

Proclamation, prayer and intercession, and the call to repentance are necessary at this time. Christians should be in prayer and intercession on behalf of our country, even as Abraham interceded for Sodom. We should demonstrate God's love amid these difficult times and conduct ourselves honorably. Those who are determined to hate God and His people may still reject us and the message no matter how palatable we make it. But we must proclaim God's Word in wisdom and love, whether we bear reproach or honor.

53

Means of Deception

Areas Where Christians Should Beware

Beloved, do not believe every spirit, but test the spirits whether they are of God; because many false prophets have gone out into the world.

—1 John 4:1

T HIS CHAPTER IS IMPORTANT BECAUSE OF THE ASSAULT THAT IS occurring against the Bible and the person and work of Jesus Christ in many so called "Christian institutions." It deals with two areas where the enemy of our souls is crafty and works subtly to deceive. The first section deals with "feel-good" experiences that cause undiscerning Christians to accept error. The second section deals with deceptive approaches to Scripture that are being used to lead astray the unwary and gullible soul. My purpose here is not to debate the unbeliever nor to convince the skeptic. My purpose is to help Christians to be aware of these potential snares and pitfalls that are prevalent in our culture today.

"Feel-Good" Experiences That Can Mislead and Deceive

Some of the experiences listed below can be true and godly if they are the fruit of the Word of God and the work of the Holy Spirit. But they can be counterfeited and used to deceive if they are not based on the written Word of God and the biblical testimony of the person and work of Jesus Christ. The experiences listed below cannot be used alone to judge whether or not something is of God.

Warm Fuzzies

The warm fuzzies can be deceptive. Emotions and sentimentality are useful but cannot be the final arbiter of what is of God. Warm thoughts and mushy feelings can be produced by good things or bad things. The soul of man without God can rejoice in evil and be infatuated with things that are not good. Emotions can deceive. Ignorance can deceive. It is possible for people to feel good about things that are ungodly and wrong.

False Peace

Passivity and quietness of the soul can also be deceptive. Israel's prophet warned those who were at ease in Zion not to be complacent in their sin. True peace comes only from a clear conscience before God. Apart from the blood of Jesus Christ and forgiveness of sin, all pseudo-peace is deceptive and fleeting. I think this is why so many people have to be drunk and party through the night. It's frightening to be alone in the dark with your thoughts when you do not know the peace that comes only from knowing Jesus and being in right-standing with God.

Relationships and Community

Many cults present a sense of belonging and "family" but tend towards control and loss of individual freedom. These "communities" tend toward bondage and legalism, or to license and immorality. The typical church has failed badly in the area of relationships and real community. This is an area where the Church needs major revelation and drastic change. Programs, agenda-driven meetings, and the theater-style settings do not meet the people's need for real fellowship in a living room setting where they can get to really know one another and develop real relationships. The shallow relationships that exist in so many churches have made many people vulnerable to the community life offered in many cults and heretical groups.

Mystical and Spiritual Experiences

The devil and false religions often produce mystical experiences, but which have their source in evil spirits, often masquerading as good spirits. The New Age influence in our culture has provided a platform for people to delve into spiritual things while avoiding the God of the Bible who requires moral accountability. This is the grounds for demonic activity in the lives of people.

Supernatural Experiences

The devil can do signs and lying wonders. This is seen in psychic activities, sorcery, meditation, animism, idol worship, Eastern religions, and the New Age movement. These practices are counterfeits of the genuine gifts of the Holy Spirit as taught and modeled in Scripture. The foundation for the supernatural is Jesus, the Bible, and the Church. The biblical context for the supernatural is that it be under the lordship of Jesus Christ, following the pattern and guidelines given in the Bible and in the context of the Church (those who follow Jesus Christ as Lord and walk according to His written Word).

Leaders Who Appear Intelligent, Gifted, and Caring

Obviously, these characteristics are good and expected in leaders. But these traits alone cannot be trusted. It is dangerous to ignore a leader's position regarding Scripture and the person and work of Christ while accepting him because he is a "nice guy," a good speaker, and loves people. Paul warns us that Satan's false prophets are like wolves in sheep's clothing; they transform themselves to appear as angels of light. The test is: Does the leader believe the Bible is the true word of God? Does he believe that Jesus Christ died for our sins and rose again as Lord? Is his moral life exemplary?

What's worse than a wolf in sheep's clothing is a wolf in shepherd's clothing.

Four Deceptive Approaches to Scripture

"Interpretation"

The Bible is rich in depth and layers of truth, but it does not have many interpretations. The Word is true as presented. When people try to interpret the Bible, they are usually trying to avoid the apparent word, principle, or command that is given. The Apostle Peter said, "...knowing this first, that no prophecy of Scripture is of any private interpretation, for prophecy never came by the will of man, but holy men of God spoke as they were moved by the Holy Spirit" (2 Pet. 1:20–21). The Bible was given to us by God Himself. It has definite, clear, and absolute meaning. It is to be taken at face value.

"Is it to be taken literally?"

People who make an issue of literality are usually avoiding the issue of truth. People who say the Bible can't be taken literally are actually saying they do not believe it is true. Again, this question is often used to avoid accepting certain truths or principles or commands that are given. I believe the Bible is true.

"It contains the word."

This concept has been taught in liberal seminaries. Basically, it means that the actual written text of the Bible, its history, stories, and messages are not necessarily fact and are not in themselves the word of God. They say the Bible is not the word of God, but rather contains the word of God. This heresy allows people to ignore the obvious truth of Scripture and simply draw from it whatever they feel God might be saying in it.

This allows people to ignore the obvious message and find something more palatable to their tastes.

"Being Selective with Scripture"

This is the belief that we can be selective or pick which parts of the Bible we choose to accept as legitimate. Leaders of heretical groups often use this tactic. This is an arrogance that allows us to judge the Bible instead of allowing it to judge us.

A milder version of this problem is seen with Christians who do believe the Bible, but who consciously or unconsciously discard Bible verses that don't fit their doctrine on certain issues. In finding biblical truth, Christians should consider all the verses related to any topic and formulate a doctrine that encompasses all the verses that speak to the subject, even the verses they might not understand or verses they might have difficulty with.

Conclusion

We are obligated and commanded to test the spirits and discern false teachers. It is so sad that too many Christians and churches do not have enough spiritual life, knowledge of Scripture, and discernment to recognize the false teachers that present themselves as angels of light. The person and work of Jesus Christ and the written Word of God must be the standard by which our intuition and discernment make judgments and determine what is of God and what is not of God. All other evidences of truth can be imitated and counterfeited.

We cannot deny the Scripture and claim to believe and obey God. The New Testament has many exhortations to know and believe God's written Word. It is also filled with admonitions and warnings about ignoring it, despising it, or twisting it. You cannot hide or escape the true and real Word of God. It will not be indifferent to you, and it is a mistake to think you can be indifferent to it. You might laugh at it, despise it, underestimate it, and think it is gone. But it will come back, and it will overtake you ... either in your surrender or in your judgment.

> For if you believed Moses, you would believe me; for he wrote about Me. But if you do not believe his writings, how will you believe My words? (John 5:46–47)

But he said to him, "If they do not hear Moses and the prophets, neither will they be persuaded though one rise from the dead." (Luke 16:31)

...our beloved brother Paul, according to the wisdom given to him, has written to you, as also in all his epistles, speaking in them of ... things hard to understand, which untaught and unstable people twist to their own destruction, as they do also the rest of the Scriptures. (2 Pet. 3:15–16)

54

Loyalty Issues

Misguided Loyalty

LOYALTY CARRIES THE IDEA OF FIDELITY AND DEVOTION. IT IS A good character trait, but its virtue, or lack of it, depends upon the object of its allegiance. Loyalty can be misplaced or misguided. It is abused when being loyal requires a person to act contrary to conscience, integrity, or truth. Misguided loyalty often stems from an attempt to avoid disfavor, rejection, or accusations of betrayal from a leader who is unwilling to really listen and who refuses to acknowledge his guilt or face issues, defects, and errors in in his life.

We should be loyal to our friends and our leaders, but loyalty does not remove our need to stay in the realm of reality and to speak the truth in love. Loyalty does not mean indulging the sin and weaknesses in those we follow or supporting the sin in our friends or fellow workers. Loyalty does not mean never having a dissenting opinion. True biblical loyalty does not mean closing your eyes to reality and failure to speak up in order to avoid disfavor. Faithful are the wounds of a friend. Open rebuke is better than secret love. Integrity, reality, and honesty are important ingredients in real love and in healthy loyalty.

Loyalty Within the Council

There should be love, harmony, wisdom, and prophetic insight in a council of church leaders. A group of elders should respect their senior leader, especially if he has been their spiritual father and mentor and give him the honor and courtesy due his position. However, individuals on any form of leadership council should speak up in their official positions and not be yes-men. Any leadership council is useless unless its members bring their wisdom and thoughts into the conversation and decisions that have to be made. It is not good when a senior pastor or leader creates an atmosphere in which the other leaders feel they are betraying him if they disagree or express concerns that need to be dealt with. A silent council is no council.

Charges of Betrayal

A couple who was rejected by their pastor left the church wounded and hurting. They were bewildered that there was no follow-up communication from people (in the church) whom they considered to be their best friends. No one called to say, "Are you okay? How are you doing? Where did you go?" Years later, they received an apology from one of those friends saying he and his wife had wanted to reach out to them but were afraid the pastor would see it as betrayal.

Ahimelech the priest of Nob would have had the same fear had he been aware of King Saul's condition. He innocently befriended David, not knowing David was fleeing from Saul. Saul, in self-pity and insecurity and grasping to hold his position, counted as enemies anyone who befriended David. He, therefore, erroneously charged Ahimelech and eighty-five priests of Nob with betrayal and executed all of those innocent men along with their families. Saul here is an example of the insecure leader who demands blind "loyalty" and perceives kindness to his "enemies" as an act of betrayal.

I know life is complicated. There are good, faithful, and godly leaders who have suffered abuse at the hands of rebellious followers. There is a time for church discipline. But this principle has been abused in the hands of a self-centered, self-righteous, and stubborn leadership. Leaders should stand in the fear of God, knowing that injustice has two sides—freeing the guilty and oppressing the innocent.

Sons of Zeruiah

Joab and Abishai, two of Zeruiah's three sons, showed themselves fiercely loyal to David in fighting David's enemies. But this outward zeal to defend David masked an inner spirit of error that manifested itself in their presumptuous and independent action. Abishai tried to get David to kill Saul when Saul was in a vulnerable position relieving himself in a cave. Joab acted contrary to David's orders and assassinated Abner and Amasa, former enemies of David whom David had pardoned and given positions of honor. Joab also slew the rebellious Absalom against David's explicit command.

The irony is that Joab later defected to King Solomon's brother, Adonijah (who desired the throne). That wickedness of heart that had previously expressed itself in a vengeful loyalty to David later caused Joab to be deceived into a misplaced loyalty to Adonijah and into the very betrayal and rebellion he had disdained in others. The "Sons of Zeruiah" will be fiercely loyal to you today … but will betray you tomorrow. We need to beware of carnality in the spirit of those who support us. For that very carnality may become a door for their own deception causing them to turn on us later.

David said, "What have I to do with you, sons of Zeruiah?" (2 Samuel 16:10). Leaders should expect their followers to walk in the Spirit and not in the flesh, even as they require it of themselves.

Loyal to the Lord

Jesus knew what it was to have faithful and loyal disciples. He also knew what it was to have ostensible followers who turned and walked away when He gave a hard word or did not respond according to their fancy. He knew what it was to be betrayed and to have friends forsake Him in the hour of trouble. But He always loved them and sought their best interest. Loyalty was important, but He did not use loyalty as a means to manipulate or "use" people.

55

Manipulation and Control

Unhealthy Control of Communication

THIS CHAPTER DEALS WITH A COUPLE OF PROBLEMS SEEN IN LEADership. The issues are principles I learned while serving as referee in a couple difficult situations and were originally written with the intention of helping pastors understand these issues that get them into trouble. Initially, I was reluctant to share these with a broader audience but then realized the principles are apropos to any discussion of healthy leadership. Many readers will identify with the problems discussed.

For every issue there is a flip side. There is always the "other side of the coin." This "flip side" issue is especially true for some of the areas covered in this article. For example, pastors usually teach on gossip, and they legitimately try to prevent unhealthy and destructive communication within their community of believers. But my emphasis here is the other side of the issue, which is leadership's unhealthy control of communication among members.

Control of Communication Among Members

A typical dilemma for leadership is how to create an atmosphere of open and healthy communication while discouraging gossip and destructive talk. There is such a thing as the scorner and the gossip whose tongues can damage good fellowship, but even in a healthy group, there are issues and concerns that need to be addressed from time to time. Leadership needs wisdom in this arena. Forbidding people to talk (restricting communication) can be a form of manipulation and a means of isolating people in order to control them. There are verses in the Bible that warn us of gossip and of the discord created by loose and uncontrolled tongues, but leaders have often used this principle to stifle necessary communication and not allow people to have free communication among themselves when genuine concerns or controversial issues arise that should be scrutinized and honestly evaluated. People should be free to communicate openly on issues that arise within the group, and individuals should have the freedom to communicate their concerns and complaints. The problem here is that leaders often exhort people to not talk, while the leadership itself fails to provide a genuine, honest, realistic, and healthy platform to deal with the real issues.

Speaking the Truth in Love

The Apostle Paul tells us we should speak the truth in love (Eph. 4:15). With this statement, he points out three operative principles that are necessary in healthy relationships. "To speak" means that people should communicate rather than suppressing real issues and concerns. It is not healthy to not speak. The error in leadership is that they often think that it is spiritual for people simply to not speak. And so they work at keeping people quiet rather than getting all the cards on the table and dealing with the realities, whatever they are. A wise man once told me that God gives us grace for reality, not for pretend.

The second and third principles are to speak "truth" and to do so "in love." It is not hard to get people to speak, but it can be difficult to get them to do it in a godly manner. This is probably why leaders can be nervous about encouraging communication. The tongue can set the world on fire, but still, communication is necessary for a healthy community.

Providing a Platform for Communication

I think it is interesting to note here that one real problem in leaders who have control issues is that they fail to provide a platform for individuals on their leadership teams to communicate their real concerns or talk about the real issues that bother them. One tool used in this form of manipulation is to plan such full agendas and organize the meetings so that the individual council members have no opportunity to "let their hair down" and share their hearts. It is possible for every member of a council or board to sit there with a shared concern over a particular issue but remain silent because the head of the group would not include or allow the topic in the agenda. The other aspect of this strategy is that leaders condemn individuals if they talk with each other individually outside the council. As a result, the real concerns of people are never addressed in or outside the councils, and the consequences will be a continual stream of frustrated people who eventually leave the church.

The Openness of a Healthy Group

In an atmosphere where people are intimidated into silence, they become unwilling or unable to speak up and fail to discuss genuine or perceived issues that are important to them. This becomes a potential volcano waiting to erupt as frustrations develop over time.

Unspoken and suppressed problems remain unresolved problems. They build up pressure and may eventually become explosive. Insecurity and lack of integrity create a closed atmosphere where people are afraid to talk. This is an unhealthy protectionism in leaders. It is based on suspicion and distrust of people. It assumes they will always do the worst if they have access to facts and information. In a healthy group where there is integrity, life, and security, there will be an atmosphere of freedom and openness. People will be able to speak the truth in love, which aids in the growth of the individual and the group.

The tongue can "set things on fire," but leadership needs to remember that some issues and problems are real. Leadership falls into serious trouble when it views the discussion of a problem as being in itself the problem. This is often an evasive action that diverts attention away from the real issues and causes the real concerns to not be addressed properly. When problems arise, they do not go away by suppressing them. Problems and complaints need to be faced and addressed. It is a mistake to evade people's concerns and attack them for "talking." If someone complains that there is a rattlesnake in the Sunday school, you need to at least check the room and make sure there is no snake hiding in a corner before you condemn the person for talking about it.

Manipulation in Leadership

Too often leaders are guilty of manipulation. Manipulation is unhealthy in any relationship and is a violation of trust. It involves the dishonest use of influence to get people to do what you want them to do and is an underhanded means of controlling people. Leaders use manipulation when they lack the ability to lead by inspiration, when they have ulterior or hidden motives, or when they are trying to get people to do what the individuals most likely would not do if they had access to all the facts. Manipulation involves giving partial truth and withholding information that would be necessary for others to make an objective decision. It means distributing information selectively, giving little twists to the facts, and sharing only that which would cause other people to respond favorably to the objectives being presented.

Diplomacy and Truth

Being diplomatic can "put a sweet face" on manipulation. Diplomacy in its positive sense refers to the ability to handle affairs in such a way as to arouse the least hostility, the ability to deal with people wisely in such a way as to stir up the least amount of conflict. This is consistent with Proverbs' wisdom which exhorts us to control our spirit, guard our tongue, and to speak wisely without stirring up unnecessary strife. This can be a good characteristic in leadership. However, we must also remember that diplomacy disassociated from truth becomes manipulation. A leader who is being diplomatic in his pursuit of peace must be careful lest he become less than honest in dealing with people. A lie that makes people feel better is still a lie. A leader must adhere to truth and reality in working with people. He should not stretch the truth, give half-truths, or lie in order to pacify or to get what he wants.

Manipulation: A Lack of Integrity and a Lack of Faith

Manipulation in leadership represents a failure at honesty and sincerity. It is an absence of faith in the Sovereign God to accomplish His work by the Spirit of God. It is a lack of faith in God's ability to work in other people. It is also a failure to respect other people.

Godly leaders lead by influence, example, and truth and not by manipulation. People follow good leaders because they trust them. Many people were offended by Jesus, but they were offended by truth. Jesus never lied or misled people to get them to do what He wanted. It is not God's will that integrity be sacrificed for vision. If the vision is of God, then God will fulfill it in His time and in His way. When leaders have to sacrifice integrity to get people to "do the right thing" then the leaders are off track.

Leadership should always remember that obtaining objectives by the use of specious arguments (those which appear sound and correct without really being so) only creates the illusion of success. Sooner or later, reality will come to light, and people will be upset.

Godly leadership requires reality and spiritual substance in those who lead. People of spiritual depth, integrity, and truth do not have to manipulate. They are willing to trust God to inspire people to do the right thing, and they are willing to let the vision fail rather than use the enemy's methods to get the job done.

56

Perspective on Grace, Works, Faith, Obedience, and Repentance

Terms That Stand in Contrast
But Not in Contradiction

A Challenge from Friends

I HAD FOUR SEPARATE CONVERSATIONS WITH FRIENDS THAT CAUSED me to have concern with some of the doctrinal trends that have been developing in the church over recent years.

One friend was telling me that, under the New Covenant, Christians do not have to repent. Grace has brought forgiveness, and a believer does not have to repent of sins.

A second friend was telling me that the terms "obey" and "obedience" were part of the Old Testament Law and are, therefore, not appropriate for the New Testament Christian.

A third friend expressed concern over my sermon titled "The Blessing Is On the Other side of Obedience," saying that this message undermined faith.

On a fourth occasion, a friend expressed a mild disapproval at my teaching on "travail and labor in intercession." His implication was that travail seemed to suggest "works" rather than faith.

The error in my friends' approaches is that their positions rested on one facet of a biblical truth overemphasized to the exclusion of other legitimate aspects. In formulating any biblical doctrine, one should look at all the Scripture verses related to the subject, those you like and those you don't like, and then formulate a doctrine that draws a circle inclusive of all those verses. Our foundation must be the whole Bible, not just one pet principle. Neither should it be only one facet of any one truth.

Faith and Travail

The following terms are interrelated: grace, faith, work, travail, obedience, and repentance.

We are looking here at biblical concepts that work together in harmony. These virtues are foundational aspects of Christian character and effectiveness. They are perfectly compatible with each other and work harmoniously together. They may stand in contrast, but they do not stand in contradiction or opposition.

For instance, "laboring in prayer" does not contradict "faith in prayer." The Apostle Paul speaks of praying with "all prayer" (Ephesians 6:18). This means there are many patterns in prayer. It can sometimes be a simple word of faith, ask and believe, or sometimes a more protracted supplication, or even intense labor and travail. All are done in faith, and we see all in the life of Jesus. He sometimes simply spoke a word of faith to get something accomplished. But then He also "offered up prayers and supplications, with vehement cries and tears" (Heb. 5:7). There is a place for both. Paul said that Epaphras labored fervently in prayer (Col. 4:12). The disciples could usually cast out demons with a word but also encountered situations in which the demons came out only by prayer and fasting (Mark 9:29).

Situations that require patience do not indicate a lack of faith. Hebrews speaks of "faith and patience" (Heb. 6:12). They work together.

Obedience does not mean salvation by works. By the same token, salvation by grace does not remove our need to obey. And salvation by faith does not remove our need to work. "Laboring in prayer" does not mean a works/merit mentality. Laborers are called into the harvest. We labor, travail, fight in prayers in the same way as we labor in the harvest (Matt. 9:38, John 4:38, Col.4:12).

Labor itself is not contrary to grace. Paul said that grace labors (1 Cor. 15:10). We labor and work, even as Jesus did. It is part of our service. But we do not work to earn salvation, which is by grace through faith, and not of works.

Obedience

Grace does not remove obedience as part of the Christian's life. Obedience is not just associated with law and rules, but in the Christian life, obedience is a dynamic of relationship. Even in the New Testament, we obey God, our Master and Lord. We obey Him and keep His word. Obedience is an element of relationship, a vital expression of our walk with Jesus Christ.

Obedience existed before the law. While obedience is also associated with law, it also exists apart from law. Obedience was a living and vital part of relationship long before there was the law. In our relationship with the Lord, we obey Him, and we obey His voice as well as His written Word.

Adam "disobeyed" (Rom. 5:19) before there was ever a "law." He disobeyed the Father.

Abraham obeyed long before there was the law. His obedience in offering Isaac was not to a law, but to a command or word arising in his relationship and communication with God (Heb. 11:8, 17).

The rich young ruler's disobedience was not to law but was a refusal to obey a word arising in his relationship with Jesus. It is interesting that in this case, it was easier for the young man to obey the law than to obey the voice of Jesus. He claimed to have kept the law from his youth but was now unable to obey Jesus' personal instructions to him. The lesson is that in your relationship with Jesus, He might ask you a hard thing. We must keep God's written Word, but we must also live a life of obedience in our relationship with Him.

Jesus obeyed the Father. He was obeying His Father's voice (Heb. 5:8, John 8:55). (He was not "under law," but nevertheless, His actions never broke His Father's law). Like Jesus, we obey the Father and the Holy Spirit. Being led by the Spirit, we fulfill the law; we do not destroy it.

> ...though He was a Son, yet He learned obedience by the things which He suffered. And having been perfected, He became the author of eternal salvation to all who obey Him. (Heb. 5:8–9)

> And being found in appearance as a man, He humbled Him-
> self and became obedient to the point of death, even the death
> of the cross. (Phil. 2:8)

He was obeying the Father ... not a law. Although the Scripture prophesied that *He* would go to the cross, there was no law that commanded Him
to do this. He was obeying the Father, not a rule. Sometimes the voice of
the Father asks us to do a hard thing, sometimes something more difficult
than anything in the law.

Luke 18:18–30

The law did not tell the rich young ruler to sell everything and follow Jesus.
But the voice of Jesus told him to do that. The young man testified that he
had "kept the law." But now was unwilling to obey the voice.

The law did not tell Abraham to offer up his son, but the voice of the
Father did tell him. (The voice also stopped him.) He obeyed the voice, the
voice that sometimes tells us to do a hard thing. To say "we are not under
the law" does not relieve us of our responsibility to obey the voice of God
and to obey His commands as Jesus told us to do. That voice will not allow
us to do evil, and it will not always lead us into soft places and comfort.

The New Testament is filled with verses using the word "obedience"
and "command." Peter's writings alone include ten sections of Scripture
using the word "obey" or "obedience" or "obedient." The New Testament
has commands, and we are told to obey the Word of God.

Repentance

Grace does not remove the need for repentance. The Great Commission
commands repentance. Even Christians are commanded to repent when
there is sin in their lives. I have a list of eighteen New Testament verses of
scripture which speak of repentance. There are more. I list here only a few
of them.

Jesus, in the Great Commission, told the disciples to go into all the
world and preach the gospel, *"teaching them to observe all things I have commanded you" (Matt. 28:20)*.

In Luke 24:47, He commanded that *"repentance ... Should be preached in
His name to all nations."*

In Jesus' message to the seven churches in the first three chapters of Revelation, he commanded them saying, *"Repent, or I will remove your lampstand"* (Rev. 2:5, paraphrased).

The Apostle Paul in his message to Athens said that God now *"commands all men everywhere to repent"* (Acts 17:30).

> But be doers of the word, and not hearers only, deceiving yourselves. For if anyone is a hearer of the word and not a doer, he is like a man observing his natural face in a mirror; for he observes himself, goes away, and immediately forgets what kind of man he was. But he who looks into the perfect law of liberty and continues in it, and is not a forgetful hearer but a doer of the work, this one will be blessed in what he does. (James 1:22–25)

57

Trusting God's Wisdom and Love

THIS CHAPTER IS FOR YOU IF YOU'VE EVER BEEN TEMPTED TO THINK that God is not treating you fairly. Looking through the veil of our flesh, we often mistakenly question God's goodness, and we especially question or doubt His wisdom. One of the foundation blocks of our faith is knowing that God is not only all-powerful and good but that He has made His redemption and grace abound to us in all wisdom and understanding. He is all-wise and righteous in all His judgments. And that applies to how He deals with us individually.

The verses below express God's right of ownership and decision-making over our lives as His servants. The example of the complaining servants warns us of the spiritual danger of envy and the error of comparing ourselves with others and making negative value judgments against the Lord based on our limited and finite knowledge. We must trust not only the goodness of God but also the wisdom of God. He is not unrighteous to forget our labor and our obedience. This chapter contains valuable lessons for all who labor in the Master's vineyard.

> And when those came who were hired about the eleventh hour, they each received a denarius. But when the first came, they supposed that they would receive more; and they likewise received each a denarius. And when they had received it, they complained against the landowner, saying, "These last men have worked only one hour, and you made them equal to us who have borne the burden and heat of the day." But he answered one of them and said, "Friend, I am doing you no wrong. Did you not agree with me for a denarius? Take what is yours and go your way. I wish to give to this last man the

same as to you. Is it not lawful for me to do what I wish with my own things? Or is your eye evil because I am good?" (Matt. 20:9–15)

"Hey, it's not fair!"

The workers who worked all day complained because those who worked only the last hour were paid first and received the same amount as those who worked all day. The reverse order of payment and the equal pay for unequal work hours exposed the hearts of those who worked longest. Their grumbling was rooted in self-centeredness, wrong motives, and blindness to the heart and character of the landowner. His kindness to the late starters was being interpreted as mistreatment of the all-day workers. This illustrates man's tendency to despise the riches of God's goodness when it is poured out on others. In our short-sightedness, we become envious and think we are deprived.

God's economy is not limited to this temporary, natural age. His rewards are both now and in eternity. When we, in our short-sighted self-centeredness, judge God's goodness and wisdom only by what we see in time (the temporal, natural perspective) we do seriously err. Men's hearts are exposed when they judge God by the "wage and hour" mentality. Such attitudes reflect self-centeredness, lack of spiritual perception, and blindness to Jesus Himself and to the Sovereignty of God.

"But I was being good when they were being bad!"

I had friends and acquaintances who were still rebellious teenagers when I was seeking God and preaching the gospel as a young boy in high school and throughout my college years. These men now have significant and thriving ministries while I sit in relative obscurity and in what has, at times, felt like relative failure. I had to deal with a subtle jealousy regarding this but have come to the place where I genuinely rejoice in God's blessing over the lives and ministries of these friends and acquaintances.

It is God's prerogative to bless whom He chooses based on His wisdom and purpose. He is Sovereign Ruler over the temporal affairs of man. He chooses and apportions, and we must trust Him with how He disposes and rewards. We must rejoice when God blesses others. We praise the Lord when we are hidden in His quiver (Isa. 49:2), while others are being used in the spotlight.

Peter: "Lord, what about that man?"

Jesus: "What is that to you? You follow me." (John 21:21–22)

We should not make value judgments about ourselves by comparing our lot to that of others or by judging our place in God according to how He treats other people. This leads to pride and arrogance if our lot is better or to envy and jealousy if our lot is worse. In any case, it leads to erroneous thinking. God deals with each of us according to His own purpose and wisdom. He does not operate on the "fairness" principle. He does according to what is right and necessary according to what He has purposed in Himself.

Worker: "But I have borne the burden and the heat of the day!"

Jesus: "Friend, I am doing you no wrong." (Matt. 20:12-13)

It is common for people to feel they have not received adequate compensation or reward for their labor and efforts. We must remember that our labor is not in vain and that our just reward is with Him (Isa. 49:3–4). It might also be good to ask ourselves if we really have born the heat of the day. I may have worked hard, but still, it is a matter of perspective. To the lazy man, every way is hard, and to the self-centered person, every task is an inconvenience and sacrifice. Often the ones who complain the hardest are those who do the least.

When we have done everything we should do, still we have done no more than was our duty to do in our relationship with God. Do we think we have given so much? What do we have that we did not receive? We have nothing that did not first originate with God. He is the source, the means, and the end. He is the center, not us. And we owe Him everything, including our lives.

"Take what is yours and go your way." (Matt. 20:15)

The complaining workers received "what was theirs" but were sent on their way. They walked away, not knowing the future blessings they had forfeited, and they were of no further use to the master. They were grasping for wages rather than looking to the rewards that come with the master's favor. Instead of focusing on the meager and limited portion we think we have earned, we should humbly serve and look to the loving Master who plans to pour on us by grace a bountiful supply from the riches of His storehouse, a supply greater than anything we could ever earn. We do not want Jesus to "give us what is ours" and then tell us to "go our way." We do not want Him to give us our request, but send leanness to our souls (Ps. 106:15). It would be the greatest loss and the cause of the deep regret to take what is "mine" and yet lose Him and the blessing of intimate fellowship with Him. He rewards faith and obedience. He Himself is our exceedingly great reward.

"I have served all these years, and you never did that for me!" (Luke 15:29)

We should rejoice when others are blessed. God does not detract from nor rob from me when He shows goodness to others. It is an evil heart that assumes God's blessing on others represents something taken from me. The elder brother in the prodigal son story was not motivated by love. He was envious and was probably afraid that the father would take away some of his inheritance and give it to the prodigal brother who had returned empty-handed after wasting his own. We must remember that the Father has unlimited wealth and increase. He would be able to restore the prodigal brother without "taking away" from the elder brother. But in any case, we should be willing to sit in a humble station and rejoice when God blesses someone we think does not deserve it. It is not proper to begrudge God's benevolence shown to others or to think we deserve it more. We should not forget what the father said to the elder brother: "Son, you are always with me, and all that I have is yours" (Luke 15:31).

"They complained..." (Matt. 20:11)

The workers acted like they were part of a union organized to protect themselves against management. God is the Sovereign Master who really loves us. We don't have to negotiate for our benefits. He has already given us all things in Christ. We serve Him, knowing that in His great love, knowledge, and wisdom, He is acting for His purpose and our good. It is our self-centeredness that makes us complain and charge Him with inequity. When we make ourselves the center (instead of God and His purpose), we darken and distort our discernment, our interpretation, and our understanding.

"Friend, I am doing you no wrong." (Matt. 20:13)

God's ways are infinitely higher than ours. He acts according to His will and purpose which are based on His perfect and complete knowledge and upon His incomprehensible wisdom and goodness. We humans are foolish to charge Him with evil. The prophet Daniel said that "the Most High rules in the kingdom of men, and gives it to whomever He pleases" (Dan. 4:25). The Apostle Paul said so eloquently, "Oh, the depth of the riches both of the wisdom and knowledge of God! How unsearchable are His judgments and His ways past finding out!" (Rom 11:33). Therefore, we must trust Him with all our heart.

More from Billy Long

THE FIRST CHRISTIANS "went out and preached everywhere, the Lord working with them and confirming the Word through accompanying signs" (Mark 16:20). The book of Acts is filled with examples of God's intimate presence and involvement in the life of the early Church. The Holy Spirit anointed the gospel message and presented Jesus Christ alive to those who heard the good news. The sick were healed, demons were cast out, and the dead were raised. The Church, with convincing power, bore witness to the resurrection of the Lord Jesus Christ.

The objective of this book is to inspire the reader to hunger for and experience the presence of God in the same way as the first Christians in the Book of Acts. The lessons and examples presented in this book are not simply academic in nature but were experienced in the author's life as a pastor and minister working with people over the years.

Part One defines and explains the gifts and supernatural manifestations of the Holy Spirit and gives first-hand testimonials. Part Two helps the reader to understand the prophetic ministry as practiced in the lives of the first Christians. Part Three gives a clear teaching to help the reader understand praying in tongues and its role in aiding the believer in a deeper experience of intercessory prayer and praise. A careful reading of this book will bring clarity and remove misconceptions relating to the role of spiritual gifts, prophesying, and tongues in the New Testament Church. Purchase your copy at www.billylongministries.com.